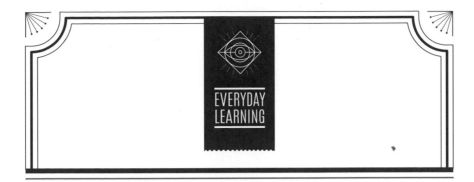

EVERYDAY LEARNING

EVERYDAY ECONOMICS
— MADE EASY —

A QUICK REVIEW OF WHAT YOU FORGOT YOU KNEW

GRACE WYNTER

WELLFLEET
PRESS

Inspiring | Educating | Creating | Entertaining

Brimming with creative inspiration, how-to projects, and useful information to enrich your everyday life, quarto.com is a favorite destination for those pursuing their interests and passions.

10 9 8 7 6 5 4 3 2 1

ISBN: 978-1-57715-235-4

Library of Congress Control Number: 2021948792

Publisher: Rage Kindelsperger
Creative Director: Laura Drew
Managing Editor: Cara Donaldson
Senior Editors: John Foster and Katharine Moore
Cover and Interior Design: Amelia LeBarron

Printed in China

INTRODUCTION 4

PART I: IN THE BEGINNING 6
CHAPTER 1: **A BRIEF HISTORY OF ECONOMIC THOUGHT** 7
CHAPTER 2: **ECONOMIC SYSTEMS** 18

PART II: UNDERSTANDING THE BASICS 23
CHAPTER 3: **BASIC ECONOMIC PRINCIPLES** 24
CHAPTER 4: **THE PRODUCTION POSSIBILITIES CURVE** 41

PART III: THE ECONOMIC DYNAMIC DUO:
MICROECONOMICS AND MACROECONOMICS 47
CHAPTER 5: **DEMAND** 48
CHAPTER 6: **SUPPLY** 59
CHAPTER 7: **CONSUMER THEORY** 68
CHAPTER 8: **MACROECONOMICS** 76
CHAPTER 9: **MONEY, INFLATION, RECESSION, AND DEPRESSION** 85
CHAPTER 10: **ECONOMIC POLICY** 97
CHAPTER 11: **THE ECONOMY'S IMPACT ON SOCIETY** 117

CONCLUSION 128

GLOSSARY 129
REFERENCES 137
ACKNOWLEDGMENTS 140
ABOUT THE AUTHOR 140
INDEX 141

INTRODUCTION

I f you're anything like me, you spent a considerable portion of your formal education questioning the real-world applications of many of your courses. But for me, economics was always different. As a college student struggling to get by with help from my parents, work study, and luck, I found that the social science of who got what and how in a society where resources were scarce appealed to me.

Fast-forward a few years and the need to understand economics feels more pressing than ever. In a time when shifting weather patterns threaten farming and food supplies across the globe, the wealth gap continues to rise, and a global pandemic stretches the limits of countries' resources, economics—the study of how society allocates its limited resources—is arguably more important than ever. The field of economics presupposes rational behavior and *ceteris paribus*, a Latin phrase that means "all other things being equal." But in a time when wearing masks to the grocery store and stocking up on toilet paper feels more rational than irrational, trying to grasp the fundamentals of economics might feel like grasping at straws.

But I believe that it's precisely during times of uncertainty that understanding the ways things work takes on greater importance. More and more, we're hearing words like "bear market," "recession," and "budget deficit" as part of the news cycle, and we have questions. Lots of them.

That's where *Everyday Economics Made Easy* comes in. Economists use data, models, and charts to help make sense of the world, some of which I'll be sharing throughout this book. Spoiler alert: Algebra actually *does* come in handy in the real world. But, no fear, the models and charts I use have been simplified to make my examples as easy to follow as possible.

I've structured this book in three sections: **In the Beginning** is where we take a brief stroll down economics memory lane so you'll understand how some early thought leaders viewed the world. In **Understanding the Basics**, I explain the types of economic systems and key concepts such as scarcity, property values, and the four factors of production. Finally, in **The Economic Dynamic Duo: Microeconomics and Macroeconomics**, I explore the key concepts in the two fields of economic study, including supply and demand, GDP, and everyone's favorite subject, taxes. And I explore social issues that affect and are affected by our economy.

I present these economic concepts in small, easily digestible pieces with the goal of maximizing your utility. If you have some familiarity with economics, you'll get that joke; if not, keep reading! What *Everyday Economics Made Easy* is not is a textbook that includes every economic theory, concept, and chart ever written. As the title suggests, it's meant to be a reference tool to help guide you through concepts you may come across in your day-to-day life.

The choices individuals, corporations, and governments make today will affect society for years to come. Understanding why these choices are being made and the impact they will have on us and our families is at the heart of this book.

If recent years have taught us anything, it's that even when we don't know what's around the corner, it's good to have a plan for it. Acquiring knowledge should be a part of that plan. Whether you've never read an economics book in your life or you majored in the subject years ago like I did, my hope is that the information in *Everyday Economics Made Easy* will become a part of the plan you make to prepare for the future.

PART
I

IN THE BEGINNING

CHAPTER 1:

A BRIEF HISTORY OF ECONOMIC THOUGHT

The **economy** refers to all the activity a society engages in with regard to producing goods and services. **Economics** is the social science that studies the allocation of scarce resources within that society. Every society operates with finite resources to produce goods and services, and economists analyze the way individuals, firms, and societies allocate these finite resources to satisfy infinite human wants.

> "Economics is a study of mankind in the ordinary business of life."
>
> —Alfred Marshall

A note here about the use of certain terms. Though our friendly neighborhood tax collectors recognize them as different entities largely based on size and structure, the words **firm**, **business**, and **corporation** are used interchangeably throughout this book because that's what we generally do in the real world. The same holds for the terms **goods** and **products** when referring to the things people buy, and **consumers** and **buyers** when we describe the people who purchase and consume goods and services.

Economists seek to make sense of the myriad decisions we make on a daily basis. They answer questions about what a society should produce, and they study the most efficient ways to produce those things. They seek to help entities in a society understand issues like inflation and unemployment, and their research helps create policies that work to solve the problems that arise from these issues.

But there hasn't always been, and isn't now, agreement about how best to address issues that affect the economy. Over the years, the field of economics has had many schools of thought.

Ancient Greek philosophers pondered issues such as property and ethics, medieval scholars wrote about the moral obligation of business to sell goods at a "just price," and mercantilists during the Renaissance were mostly concerned with furthering the national interest. Adam Smith and the industrial revolution and classical economists such as John Stuart Mill studied capitalists and workers and how they worked together toward the national good. Following World War I, Keynesian economists advocated government intervention to help stimulate growth.

— EARLY ECONOMIC THOUGHT, 750–275 BCE —

Although economics was not officially considered a discipline until the mid-nineteenth century, the allocation of resources, the concept of scarcity, and the idea of levying taxes to support economies all date back to early civilization. The Hebrew Bible speaks frequently about property and admonishes believers to be good stewards with capital.

Ancient Egyptian economy relied on agriculture and barter. There was no cash in Egyptian times, so **scribes**, under the rule of Pharaohs, levied taxes that were paid in grain, cattle, and other goods. Religion, morality, and ethics played major roles in early economic thought, with the state and well-being of the worker being of utmost importance.

The Greek Hesiod (circa 750 BCE) is one of the earliest recorded economic thinkers. The eighth-century BCE farmer and poet lived in Boeotia, where he saw the effects of scarcity on his small, agricultural community. In "Works and Days," a poem whose first 383 verses were about the scarcity of resources, Hesiod noted the importance of allocating time and materials efficiently in production while pursuing harmony and justice in society.

A Greek philosopher and student of Socrates, Plato (428–348 BCE) is known in economics for outlining the concepts of division of labor and the ideal state. Plato, who advocated strict limits on wealth, described a society where individuals were mutually dependent on each other for survival and where justice in the ideal state was equal to justice for the individual. Plato believed that individuals possessed qualities that made them better at doing certain things, and he felt that by delineating tasks, society could improve production and trade for products they were less efficient at producing.

Aristotle (384–322 BCE), a student of Plato's, is considered by many the father of **natural law**, the belief that all people have inherent rights granted to them by God. This Greek philosopher believed that people had basic needs and wants and that they went about fulfilling these in different ways. He also believed that people were born unequal and that some were destined to be subject to others. Aristotle championed the concept of private property, believing that property and wealth could help individuals live more virtuously. Unlike Plato, Aristotle championed private ownership and argued that private property promoted efficiency, unity, justice, and virtue.

In *Arthashastra* or *The Science of Political Economy*, Indian teacher and royal advisor Kautilya, also known as Chanakya (350–275 BCE), wrote on politics, military strategy, and economics, among other topics. This ancient Indian treatise addressed managing efficient economies and the ethics of economics. Kautilya espoused the concept that the state's role was to promote the economic welfare of a society, and that included providing subsidies for agriculture and trade.

The fall of Rome and the period between the fifth and twelfth centuries saw a waning in discussions of economics and economic theory. During the Middle Ages, when religion was at the forefront of society, theologian Thomas Aquinas (1225–1274) advanced the ideas of property, **just price**—a fair, mutually agreed upon price—while denouncing **usury**, the practice of lending money at unreasonably high interest rates.

– MERCANTILISM –

Though the term **mercantilism** wasn't coined until the late 1700s, the 1500s saw the rise of this economic theory that promoted governmental regulation of the economy. Mercantilists believed that increasing exports, specifically to collect precious metals, was the best way to advance a nation's wealth. The period between 1500 and 1800 saw nations levying tariffs to encourage exports and using their military power to protect local markets and supplies.

In England, Thomas Mun (1571–1641), director of the British East India Company, believed trade was the only way to increase England's wealth and advocated for reducing imports and increasing land utilization to achieve that goal. In France, minister of finance under King Louis XIV and strong proponent of mercantilism Jean Baptiste Colbert (1619–1683) levied high tariffs on foreign producers and rewarded French exporters. Colbert's program of economic reconstruction helped make France Europe's dominant power.

Mercantilism began its decline in the late eighteenth century with the advent of the industrial revolution and as people became disenchanted with mercantilist regulations.

Those disenfranchised with government regulations advocated for **laissez-faire** economics, the idea that government should be hands-off when it came to the economy. These thinkers believed that a nation's wealth was derived solely from the value of its agriculture, and that if government left the markets alone, the laws of supply and demand would naturally correct any disequilibrium.

In his book *La Physiocratie*, Samuel du Pont de Nemours, the founder of DuPont, the world's second largest chemical company, called for low tariffs and free trade. Du Pont coined the term **physiocracy**, which translates to "the rule of nature," and was among those arguing that natural economic growth would occur if governments left the markets alone.

A page from Quesnay's *Tableau Économique*

In 1758, French scientist, surgeon, and economist Francois Quesnay (1694–1774) wrote *Tableau Économique*, in which he used a single page to demonstrate how an economy functions. This analytical breakdown of the economy was considered one of the first scientific approaches to economics. In this work, Quesnay illustrated three distinct classes: landlords, farmers, and artisans and merchants, and showed the circular flow of income among them. Quesnay felt that high taxes led to poverty, and he wanted King Louis XV to cut taxes and deregulate trade to improve the French economy.

Physiocrats were among the first laissez-faire thinkers—believing that the government should take a hands-off approach to the economy, allowing it to naturally correct.

— CLASSICAL ECONOMICS —

Classical economics, or **classical liberalism**, has its roots in Britain in the late eighteenth century. John Locke (1632–1704) is known as the father of liberalism—what is widely known today as libertarianism. **Libertarianism** is a political philosophy based on the belief in governed consent of the people. In his *Second Treatise of Government*, Locke argued that not only was it the government's role to keep its hands off people's property and "lives and liberties," but also that it was the government's duty to ensure their citizens' protection. Locke felt that natural rights trumped man-made rights and that the government had no justification to take away those rights. He also wrote about the prices of goods rising and falling as a result of the number of buyers and sellers in the market and noted that that relationship was universal across all goods and services.

Scottish philosopher Adam Smith (1723–1790) is known as the second father of classical liberalism. His book, *An Inquiry into the Nature and Causes of the Wealth of Nations*, is cited as the beginning of modern Western economics. *The Wealth of Nations* offered that a country's wealth was a product of its national income, which, in turn, was a result of the division of labor and the use of capital. Smith's concept of the "invisible hand" held that unobservable market forces in a free market economy resulted in unintended benefits to society.

Jean-Baptiste Say's (1767–1832) *A Treatise on Political Economy* helped popularize Adam Smith's work in France. Say believed that, because production was the result of people fulfilling their own wants as opposed to the wants of

> # "It is not from the benevolence of the butcher, the brewer, or the baker that we expect our dinner, but from their regard to their own interest."
>
> *–Adam Smith*

ADAM SMITH
(1723–1790)

Adam Smith was born in 1723 in Kirkcaldy, Scotland. At fourteen, Smith entered the University of Glasgow on scholarship and continued his education at Balliol College at Oxford before returning to teach at Glasgow University in 1751.

An economist, author, and philosopher, Smith is known as the father of modern economics, and his book, *An Inquiry into the Nature and Causes of the Wealth of Nations* (1776), is considered the first modern work of economics. In *Wealth of*

Everett Collection/Shutterstock

Nations, Smith introduced the concept of an "invisible hand," the unseen force in a society's market that pushes demand and supply toward equilibrium, creating an efficient allocation of resources that benefits an entire society.

Smith wrote that the wealth of a nation should be measured by the total of its production and commerce, a concept now known as the **gross domestic product** (GDP). And his explanations of labor, assembly-line production, free markets, and wages are considered the foundations of a free market economy.

Smith died in 1790 at age sixty-seven. His ideas continue in the classical school of economics, and in 2007, his image was placed on the £20 note.

others, it was possible for production to exceed demand, creating a "general glut" of supply. Over time, however, the market would correct itself as businesses shifted to respond to the change in demand.

Economist and philosopher John Stuart Mill (1806–1873) put forward the concept of **utilitarianism**, a philosophy that aims to improve society as a whole, believing that actions are right if they result in increased happiness of the greatest number of people.

These classical economists championed market economies as self-regulating systems governed by the invisible hand and realized the economic value of labor as a factor in the price of producing goods and services.

– SOCIAL ECONOMISTS –

Karl Marx (1818–1883) is one of the world's most well-known social economists. Marx, who is thought to be one of the first economists to address globalization, believed in the value of labor, but criticized capitalism. In *Das Kapital*, he wrote that capitalism exploited working-class laborers. Marx argued that capitalism benefited the ruling class, allowing them to become richer at the expense of cheap labor. He favored government intervention to help ensure maximum benefits to its citizens.

Though closely related, Marxian economics and Marxism are different. **Marxian economics** focuses more broadly on the economic aspects of a society's decisions, while **Marxism**, the basis for communism, focuses on the political, social, and economic aspects of a society.

– KEYNESIAN ECONOMICS –

On January 18, 1919, World War I allies met just outside of the city of Paris to establish the terms for peace. A day later, economist John Maynard Keynes (1883–1946), who was present for the talks, left the Paris Peace Conference in protest over the signing of the Treaty of Versailles that officially ended World War I. Using data from conference records, Keynes, in his paper, *The Economic Consequences of the Peace*, accurately predicted that the treaty's harsh terms would lead to Germany's financial collapse, an event that would have far-reaching consequences across Europe and the rest of the world.

During the Great Depression that followed a decade later, Keynes advocated for lowering taxes to stimulate demand and increasing government expenditures to help pull the global economy out of the depression. Keynes's focus on **aggregate demand**—the idea that firms only produce what they expect to sell—is a foundation of Keynesian economics and the belief that government policies that influence aggregate demand can help prevent economic slumps.

– MONETARISM AND – FREE MARKET CAPITALISM

American professor, economist, and statistician Milton Friedman (1912–2006) developed numerous views that opposed Keynesian theory about free markets. One of Friedman's theories, the theory of **consumption function**, described the relationship between consumption and disposable income and introduced the idea that, all else being equal, short-term increases in income decreased savings and kept consumption static.

Building on Keynesian economics and finding somewhat different conclusions, Friedman introduced **monetarism**, which focused on banking and held that, in a society, the money supply was the chief determinant of GDP and price levels. Monetarists believe that optimal monetary policy targets the money supply's growth rate. Monetarism's popularity grew in the late 1970s when inflation peaked at 20 percent and U.S. policy shifted to reflect monetary theory.

– NEOCLASSICAL ECONOMICS –

Neoclassical economics emerged in the 1900s as a response to classical economic thinking. Unlike classical economists, who believed that production costs were the most important factors in a product's price, neoclassical economists believed that consumer perception of a good's value was the driving factor in setting its price. Neoclassical theory made the case for **utility**, the amount of satisfaction consumers received from consuming goods and services. Individuals also exchanged labor for leisure, making decisions about the incremental increases in satisfaction they gained by exchanging a resource—their labor—for another—wages.

EXAMPLES OF GLOBALIZATION

CULTURE

Employees and corporations that operate beyond their home countries take aspects of their home cultures with them and are exposed to new cultures in their new countries of residence. Examples of cultural globalization include music—think of the global impact of Bob Marley, for instance; spirituality—the Indian tradition of yoga is now widely practiced worldwide; and even language, where language-learning apps and devices facilitate people's desire to communicate in multiple languages at home and abroad.

FOOD

Food is another distinct area where globalization becomes evident with a visit to your local supermarket. International aisles feature foods and spices from all over the globe, and specialty stores and farmers' markets feature items that have traditionally been difficult to find outside of their countries of origin. The flip side is that with 37,000 McDonald's locations in about 120 countries around the world, there are only a few places in the world where you can't get your hands on their famous fries.

FAST FASHION

Globalization has meant an abundance of "fast fashion"—cheap, trendy clothes that quickly move from the design stage to retail shelves. These clothes are manufactured in countries where labor is cheap, offering low wages earned in environments with inadequate employee safety monitoring. Fast fashion also has a major impact on the environment. The dyes and textiles used to create these clothes are the second largest polluter of clean water after agriculture.

Mainstream economics is an umbrella term used to describe theories that fall into neoclassical thought. Mainstream economics accepts the invisible hand working within the market and assumes individuals behave rationally and that profit benefits all parties involved. The failure of neoclassical economics to predict the 2008 financial collapse and resulting recession has called into question the idea that the pursuit of profit always results in the common good.

DID YOU KNOW?

North Korea and Cuba are the only countries in the world where you can't buy Coca-Cola.

– PRESENT-DAY ECONOMIC THOUGHT – AND GLOBALIZATION

The International Monetary Fund (IMF) defines **globalization** as the "the process through which an increasingly free flow of ideas, people, goods, services, and capital leads to the integration of economies and societies." In a world where, according to a World Bank estimate, 9.2 percent of the population lives on less than $1.90 a day, this movement of resources around the globe has led to increasing standards of living in many low- and middle-income countries (LMICs). But the effects of globalization haven't been positive for everyone.

Globalization has existed since ancient times. The **Silk Road**, which derived its name from the silk that was traded, refers to the network of trade routes established during China's Han Dynasty that carried goods and ideas between Rome and China from 130 BCE until 1453 CE.

European expansion into the New World saw trade in food, plants, culture, and ideas. And between 1525 and 1866, 12.5 million Africans were shipped to the New World and enslaved, one of the most egregious examples of globalization in history.

Globalization allows for trade, as in when American automobile manufacturers make car parts in Mexico and North Korea. Call centers are perhaps one of the most visible examples of companies' globalization efforts, as they outsource jobs to places like India, where labor costs are cheaper. Residents of these areas benefit with higher standards of living and customers benefit by paying lower prices. But the downside includes the loss of jobs in some countries and higher income inequality between social classes.

Fiscal and monetary policies are the two ways governments address the issues of globalization and other economic factors that affect individuals and societies. The challenges these societies have in common are finding optimal ways to operate when almost all resources are limited.

In the next chapter, we'll take a look at the types of economic systems that have evolved to meet this challenge.

> **"The raw fact is that every successful example of economic development this past century— every case of a poor nation that worked its way up to a more or less decent, or at least dramatically better, standard of living— has taken place via globalization, that is, by producing for the world market rather than trying for self-sufficiency."**
>
> *—Paul Krugman*

CHAPTER 2:
ECONOMIC SYSTEMS

The way a society allocates its resources and produces, prices, and distributes its goods and services across a geographical area is its **economic system**. Economists break economic systems down into four main types: **traditional**, **command**, **market**, and **mixed**. Let's take a look at what distinguishes these systems from each other.

– TRADITIONAL –

Traditional economic systems date back to ancient times. These economies are not technologically advanced, rely on traditions, and center around family or tribal customs. They are largely dependent on agriculture, hunting, and fishing. Because few resources may be naturally available in the region, or because access to resources is limited in some way, surpluses are rare in traditional economies, and most still use bartering as a chief form of exchange.

Examples of current traditional economic systems can be seen in parts of Africa, Asia, Latin America, and the Middle East. In the United States, some Amish communities still operate under a traditional economy, eschewing technology and relying on the land to supply their needs. Anthropologists believe that most economies began as the traditional model, and for that reason, they also believe that today's traditional economies will eventually evolve into one of the other types.

– COMMAND –

In command economies, the central government makes almost all economic decisions. Ideally, in these planned economic systems, the government is able to mobilize resources in a way that provides goods, services, and employment for all capable and eligible citizens. Command economies don't rely on the laws of supply and demand that guide market economies, and they often ignore the customs that define traditional economies. A central plan sets the goals for these societies.

NORTH KOREA:
A COMMAND ECONOMY

The Democratic People's Republic of Korea (DPRK), or North Korea as it is more widely referred to, is a communist country with a command economy. In this economy, the government determines what will be produced, how much of it will be produced, and the price at which goods will be sold. According to the CIA's World Factbook, as of 2015, North Korea's GDP was estimated to be $40 billion with a per capita value of $1,800. The figure hasn't been updated since then, due in large part to the secretive nature of the North Korean government.

The country's economic challenges date back to World War II, when Japanese forces in northern Korea surrendered to the Soviet Union and American troops took charge of the southern region. In 1950, backed by the Soviet Union, North Korean leader Kim Il-Sung attempted to capture the southern region, a move that kicked off the Korean War. Following Kim Il-Sung's failed attempt to bring the entire peninsula under communist rule, North Korea followed the Soviet model of a centrally planned, socialist economy and ideology of self-reliance. Investing in steel, cement, and iron and developing heavy industry (capital-intensive businesses) were key components of this model.

Many economists believe the country's economic problems accelerated as a result of its government's emphasis on heavy industry and military-first politics. A food crisis after a series of national disasters in the 1990s further worsened its economy.

Today, North Korea's economy remains heavily nationalized: industries and assets are under government control, education and health care are free, and the state heavily subsidizes food and housing. But the country's emphasis on maintaining a defense economy has come at the expense of adequate food production, living standards, and human rights.

The government owns access to critical resources, such as oil and gas, and has a monopoly on businesses, ruling out domestic competition in these sectors. The central plan determines production quantities and pricing, and for that reason, these economies can mobilize quickly to manage large-scale projects.

In command economies, individual desires and wants take a back seat to societal needs. Because pricing and production are largely independent of consumer demand, rationing is often present in these types of systems. Command economies are essential to the operation of socialist and communist societies.

The former Soviet Union and Eastern Bloc countries were command economies, and the fall of communism in that region can partially be attributed to the inefficiencies of the command system. Other examples of command economies include North Korea (DPKR), where housing prices are low because the government owns the country's houses and sets its home prices. In Belarus, the government owns 80 percent of the country's businesses.

— MARKET —

In its simplest form, a market exists when parties exchange things of value. Your local supermarket is probably the concept of a market that's most familiar. Grocery store owners purchase goods, price them based on several factors, including production costs and competitor prices, then stock their shelves with these goods. Shoppers select the groceries they need, take them to the register or scanner, and exchange money for these goods. The stock market is another example of parties exchanging goods, in this case publicly listed companies. A market economy operates in a similar way. Firms and individuals determine the types of goods and services that are produced and set prices without government intervention.

In free market economies, the government interferes little with the economy. Households and firms make decisions, and the laws of supply and demand direct prices and the production of goods and services. Capitalist societies require free market economies to operate. Market economies have four major characteristics:

- **Property rights**—legal ownership of resources
- **Private enterprise**—the freedom to engage in economic activity
- **Prices and profits**—an efficient market where price is a reflection of demand and supply
- **Limited government**—the government ensures all of the above is taking place and penalizes entities that disobey, but does not generally set prices or production levels

Market economies help ensure that the goods and services produced are the ones that are in demand. Companies that innovate and meet consumer needs are rewarded with profits, which incentivizes them to continue to seek innovation. The term **laissez-faire**, which translates from the French as "allow to do," is one of the hallmarks of a market economy. But because market economies reward competition, it can overlook those who are less competitive, such as those with disabilities, children, and the elderly. Because most real-life economies involve some degree of government intervention, most economies are considered mixed.

KARL MARX
(1818–1883)

Philosopher, author, and social theorist Karl Marx is perhaps most famous for his ideas about capitalism and communism. Marx was born in Trier, Prussia (Germany), and was the oldest surviving son in a family of nine children. As a young man, he studied law in Bonn and Berlin, where he became involved with a group that was critical of the political and religious establishments of the day. Marx wrote for the liberal democratic newspaper *Rheinische Zeitung*, where his ideas became increasingly radical, and the Prussian government later banned the paper.

Alevtina_Vyacheslav/Shutterstock

In his 1867 work *Das Kapital*, Marx argued that societies were composed of business owners who owned the means of production and a larger class of workers, which he called the proletariat, who didn't own the means of production but provided labor in return for money. Marx believed that this arrangement exploited workers.

Vladimir Lenin and Josef Stalin used Marx's theories as the foundations for their communist rule, and Marx's ideas formed the basis of Marxism. Marx's *The Communist Manifesto* expounds on his theories about society, politics, and socialism. His ideas have had a major impact on societies, particularly communist societies, and his views on sociology and politics have remained hugely influential.

Mixed economies combine elements of the other types of economies. These economies protect property rights, are driven by the self-interest of individuals, and operate under the laws of supply and demand. But they may also set prices and operate some enterprises. Almost all the world's capitalist societies are mixed economies. The United States, for example, while allowing property rights, private enterprise, and efficient markets, establishes the minimum wage (a price floor) and enacts laws that regulate companies' abilities to set their own pricing.

In addition to ensuring adherence to things like the minimum wage, the government in a mixed economy also plays a large role in areas such as international trade, the military, social safety programs, and providing public transportation to its residents. Because a mixed economy combines elements of the other economies, it can avoid some of their disadvantages. For instance, mixed economies may fund things like defense and technology, which may receive less funding in true market economies. Mixed economies also benefit in their ability to account for less competitive members of society.

Regardless of the type of economic system a society operates within, the players include individuals, firms, and governments. Economists study individuals and firms as one field—microeconomics—and governments and societies—macroeconomics—as another.

"Without labor, nothing prospers."
–Sophocles

DID YOU KNOW?

The film adaptation of *The Grapes of Wrath* was banned in the USSR because moviegoers were shocked that even downtrodden Americans could still afford a car.

PART II

UNDERSTANDING THE BASICS

CHAPTER 3:
BASIC ECONOMIC PRINCIPLES

Microeconomics analyzes the ways in which individuals, households, workers, and for-profit businesses make decisions and allocate limited resources. The field explores concepts like supply and demand, production, property rights, consumer choices, prices, and why and how people and companies spend their money.

> ## "Economics is a choice between alternatives all the time. Those are the trade-offs."
> ### –Paul Samuelson

We'll take a deeper dive into microeconomics in the next chapter, but for now, just think about microeconomics as what happens in your household and in your neighborhood.

Where microeconomics takes a bottom-up approach to analyzing the economy, **macroeconomics** operates from the top down, studying a society's policies and actions and the ways they affect its members as a whole. Macroeconomics focuses on big-picture things like GDP, inflation, recession, unemployment, and the stock market.

Although two distinct areas of study, the fields are interrelated. Individual family decisions, like a father leaving the workforce to become a stay-at-home dad or a daughter quitting school and getting a job to help support her single mother, have a cumulative effect on a country's economy. Likewise, companies replacing human labor with machine labor not only affects a country's overall productivity but also results in the real consequence of individual households managing the aftermath of lost wages.

We make choices based on economic concepts every day, whether we realize it or not. Some, like gleefully buying a bunch of your favorite candy bars because they're on sale (prices affecting the quantity demanded) or regretting eating that fourth candy bar in one sitting (diminishing marginal utility), are relatively simple. Others can be much more complicated. The business trying to decide what combination of goods to produce to deliver the most profit (production possibilities) or a government faced with rising unemployment weighing between sending out stimulus checks (fiscal policy) or reducing the interest rate (monetary policy) are examples of more complex decisions.

To understand the reasons behind, and implications of, these real-world economic challenges, we must understand certain basic principles that apply, whether we're talking about a family, a small business, or a society. Let's begin tackling these basics by taking a look at scarcity and rivalry.

− SCARCITY −

Scarcity is the gap between what we want to consume and what's available for consumption. It's a major tenet of economics because economics is all about studying how we meet infinite demands with finite resources. If individuals, businesses, and societies had unlimited resources, questions about allocation, production, and pricing would largely be moot; we would all have everything we need all the time (which would actually present a different set of problems, but that's for a different book). But it's precisely because resources are scarce that economists study their allocation.

You might be wondering whether there are any resources that aren't scarce. Non-scarce resources, also known as free goods, are available without limit. Oxygen, for example, can be considered a free resource; contrary to what my family might lead you to believe, my consuming the air around me doesn't mean less air for the person sitting next to me, no matter how much I'm talking. But in general, most resources are scarce, and when that resource is limited, and there is more demand for it than exists, who gets that resource, how much of it can they get, and what will they have to exchange for it? These questions lead to the concept of rivalry.

SCARCITY DURING COVID-19

In March 2020, as COVID-19 rolled through the United States, medical personnel began sounding the alarm about supply shortages. N-95 masks and other personal protective equipment (PPE) like gowns and face shields, and patient necessities like ICU beds and ventilators, were in increasingly short supply. As a consequence, hospital staff and patients suffered. America was experiencing a scarcity of resources at a time when it could least afford it.

The world was experiencing scarcity as a result of increasing demand, panic buying, and a failure to restock previously depleted supplies. The World Health Organization (WHO) warned that these disruptions in the global PPE supply would endanger lives, and they called for a 40 percent increase in manufacturing.

Political leaders were faced with making difficult decisions about who needed the limited supplies of PPE the most. Medical professionals had to choose between which patients they would place on ventilators and which, they hoped, would survive without them. The scarcity affected not only first responders and those who'd contracted COVID-19, but also U.S. citizens, who began sewing their own masks to protect themselves.

And PPE wasn't the only area that experienced scarcity. Toilet paper sales skyrocketed 845 percent in early March as states announced lockdowns. COVID-19-related unemployment and school closings resulted in an increase in households reporting food scarcity (not having enough to eat).

Many of us experience scarcity of some sort on a daily basis, whether that's not having enough hours in the day to get something done or not having enough money in the bank to pay bills, and we begin learning these scarcity lessons at an early age. But when a global pandemic hits and scarcity spreads across international borders, affecting the entire world at once, the reality of scarcity takes on quite a different meaning.

— RIVALRY —

Rivalry exists when multiple parties are competing for the same thing. Rival goods and resources are things that, when consumed by one person, reduce the ability for another to consume. Rival goods can also be goods that can't be consumed simultaneously. For instance, if there's only one umbrella in a house with five people all heading to different places on a rainy day, somebody—or several bodies—are going to get wet. A bottle of water, a plane ticket, and a house are all examples of rival goods. Oxygen, public parks, radio stations, and sunlight are examples of non-rival goods: consumption by one does not reduce another's ability to consume.

Scarcity and rivalry play important roles in our everyday world and can often highlight disparities among the wealthy and poor in a society. During times of shortages, when scarcity results in increased prices on staples like food and toilet paper, those who are more financially stable are more likely to be able to obtain goods than those who are financially insecure.

EVERYDAY EXAMPLE

Let's assume an average public city bus has a capacity for thirty seated passengers and standing room for fifty-five. At 4:30 p.m. the bus rolls up to your stop, and you take one of several remaining empty seats. By the time the bus stops in front of your apartment at the end of your journey, all seats are full, and there's no standing room left. Space on the bus is a scarce resource.

The following day, a baseball game being held at the field near your bus stop ends at 4:00 p.m., and when the bus gets to your stop half an hour later, all but one of the seats are taken. As you head toward the empty seat, you realize another passenger is also headed toward the seat. In a split second, you have to decide whether to let him have the seat, engage in a spirited battle of rock-paper-scissors, or stand all the way home. You and the other passenger are both engaged in rivalry. And, in the time it took to understand this concept, the other passenger has already taken the seat.

In societies where resources are scarce, what defines their allocation and the concepts of supply and demand is the existence of property rights. Without them, market economies—systems where production and prices are determined by privately owned businesses—would be severely limited.

— PROPERTY RIGHTS —

As mentioned earlier, the United States is a mixed system because the government does not take a completely hands-off role when it comes to the economy. It gives assistance in the form of food-cost supplementation and health care to vulnerable individuals and provides incentives to businesses to produce certain types of products. Still, for a mixed economy system like the United States to function efficiently, property rights must be established and protected. Markets are efficient at producing private goods in large part because entities that own resources have the right to exchange those resources.

In mixed or market economies, **property rights** refer to laws that give entities exclusive, enforceable, and transferable ownership of resources. Private property rights include an owner's exclusive right to determine the property's use. Public land, such as parks, forests, and wilderness areas, on the other hand, is owned by the public and managed by the government.

When economists talk about property rights, they're not just talking about a house with clearly defined, white-picket-fence borders. In economic terms, **property** is anything tangible or intangible owned by private individuals or entities. In a system that honors property rights, the market value of a property reflects the demand for it from the rest of society. Property rights exist to prevent predatory competition to gain control over economic resources. Patents are also a form of property rights. These temporary, exclusive rights granted to inventors by the government exist to encourage innovation and invention while excluding others from making, using, or selling the invention for the number of years specified in the patent. Owners of property rights have the authority to determine how their property is used.

Individuals and firms can obtain property rights for:

- Tangible goods, such as land, homes, jewelry, computer hardware, and physical books
- Intangible items, such as inventions, patents, and copyrights
- Nonhumans, such as family pets and livestock

Property rights allow entities to own the resources to produce the goods and services consumers want. The creation of these goods and services depend on the four factors of production.

INTELLECTUAL PROPERTY RIGHTS AND COUNTERFEIT GOODS

We've all seen them: Gucci handbags at impossibly low prices, phones that look like iPhones but seem just a little bit off, and websites offering free downloads of expensive software or just-released novels by best-selling authors. These are examples of counterfeit and pirated items, and they infringe on the rightful owners' real and intellectual property rights.

When property rights are violated, ownership and exclusivity are abandoned with far-reaching consequences. The Office of Intellectual Property Enforcement (IPE) estimates that theft of intellectual property costs the U.S. economy $180 billion annually in theft from trade secrets and $18 billion in theft from pirated U.S. software.

The International Chamber of Commerce (ICC) reports that in 2013 the value of international and domestic trade in counterfeit and pirated goods was between $710 and $917 billion, and that digital piracy of movies and music created "an enormous drain on the global economy—crowding out billions in legitimate economic activity."

– FOUR FACTORS OF PRODUCTION –

Early economists such as Adam Smith and Karl Marx identified land, labor, and capital as the factors necessary for production, and today, those and a fourth factor, entrepreneurship, make up the four factors of production. Together, these factors produce the goods and services that profit-generating firms sell.

Factors of production are the inputs required to create a good or service. The four factors of production are:

- Land/natural resources
- Labor
- Capital
- Entrepreneurship

LAND/NATURAL RESOURCES

Land refers to natural resources such as gold, oil, timber, water, commercial real estate, and, of course, actual land. Because many natural resources are not renewable, efficiently managing them is essential in the production process. When land is processed from its original condition, it becomes a capital good.

QUICK TIP

Unrefined oil is a natural resource, but gasoline, because it is processed, is a capital good.

LABOR

Someone has to convert natural resources into goods, and the effort needed by individuals to bring a product or service to market is known as **labor**. In a free society, laborers are rewarded for their effort with income. Education, skill level, and the type of work performed are all factors that determine the amount of income laborers receive from their work.

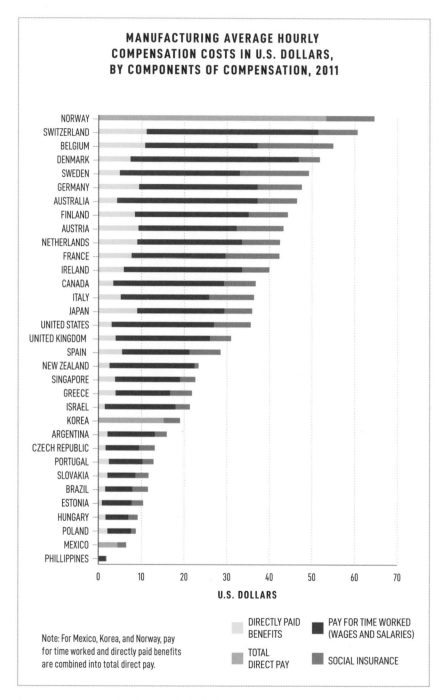

MANUFACTURING AVERAGE HOURLY COMPENSATION COSTS IN U.S. DOLLARS, BY COMPONENTS OF COMPENSATION, 2011

Countries (top to bottom): NORWAY, SWITZERLAND, BELGIUM, DENMARK, SWEDEN, GERMANY, AUSTRALIA, FINLAND, AUSTRIA, NETHERLANDS, FRANCE, IRELAND, CANADA, ITALY, JAPAN, UNITED STATES, UNITED KINGDOM, SPAIN, NEW ZEALAND, SINGAPORE, GREECE, ISRAEL, KOREA, ARGENTINA, CZECH REPUBLIC, PORTUGAL, SLOVAKIA, BRAZIL, ESTONIA, HUNGARY, POLAND, MEXICO, PHILLIPPINES

U.S. DOLLARS

Legend:
- DIRECTLY PAID BENEFITS
- PAY FOR TIME WORKED (WAGES AND SALARIES)
- TOTAL DIRECT PAY
- SOCIAL INSURANCE

Note: For Mexico, Korea, and Norway, pay for time worked and directly paid benefits are combined into total direct pay.

Source: U.S. Bureau of Labor Statistics, International Labor Comparisons

CAPITAL

Capital or **capital goods** are tangible assets like gasoline, equipment, machinery, and commercial buildings that are used to produce other goods. These man-made goods don't directly create revenue for companies because they aren't sold, but they're important to a nation's economy because they can increase efficiency and productivity. Additional examples of capital include forklift machinery, office furniture, computers, and conveyor belts. Capital as a factor of production is distinct from private capital or assets for personal use, such as money or a personal vehicle.

ENTREPRENEURSHIP

Entrepreneurship refers to the process of putting together the other factors of production to produce things, and entrepreneurs are the people and businesses who do it. Entrepreneurs rely on innovation and undertake risk to use resources to produce goods and services. In the United States, the majority of entrepreneurs are small business owners, and these small business owners make up the engine that drives their country's economic growth. According to the Small Business Administration's (SBA) Office of Advocacy 2020 Small Business Profile, the United States' 31.7 million small businesses make up 99.9 percent of U.S. businesses and employ more than 60.6 million people.

– PROFIT –

In economics, **profit** is the reward entrepreneurs receive for taking risk. The goal of most businesses in a mixed market economy is to maximize profit. Firms seek to maximize profits for the same reason individuals seek to maximize income and savings. More income and profits allow people and firms to have and do more of the things they want to.

DID YOU KNOW?

Fifty percent of all profit generated by public companies in the United States comes from thirty companies.

Profits ensure that firms, large ones like multinational corporations and small ones like your local bakery, not only produce the products and services buyers demand, but that they also continue to innovate and take on entrepreneurial risks to increase efficiency. Regardless of the size of a firm, economists calculate profits the same way. A firm's total profits equals its total revenue minus total costs.

Profit Formula: Profit = Total Revenue (TR) − Total Costs (TC)

In a market, businesses maximize profit by producing goods and services at the level where the cost of producing an additional unit of a good or service (marginal cost, MC) equals the increase in revenue generated from selling that additional unit (marginal revenue, MR). A market's structure affects a firm's ability to make a profit, so let's take a look at four types of market structures.

> ## "In general, if any branch of trade, or any division of labour, be advantageous to the public, the freer and more general the competition, it will always be the more so."
>
> *—Adam Smith*, The Wealth of Nations, *Book IV, Chapter II*

− MARKET STRUCTURES −

As we've learned, economists believe that an efficient, competitive, free market society is the most optimal way to allocate limited resources. In a capitalist society, the presence of competition compels firms to seek out the most efficient ways to produce goods and services. This competition and the relationship producers have to consumers helps define an economy's market structure.

Market structure refers to the models that identify characteristics of a market that affect its behavior and defines the relationship between buyers and sellers. There are four types of market structures: perfect competition; and monopoly, monopolistic competition, and oligopoly, which are classified as forms of imperfect competition. Knowing the differences between them can help us understand a firm's production decisions.

PERFECT COMPETITION

Perfect competition, also known as pure competition, occurs when a large number of small firms compete with each other to provide similar goods and services. Perfect competition is characterized by the following:

- There are many buyers and sellers
- There are no barriers to entry
- No single firm has a significant share of the market
- No single firm has the ability to influence market price
- Supply and demand determine what's produced and available in the market
- There isn't a major difference between competitor products
- Buyers have complete information
- Firms can enter or exit the market without capital or cost

Perfect competition is rare in the real world for several reasons. "Complete information" rarely exists in the real world, but barriers to entry, capital requirements, and product differentiation do. That said, some industries do come close. Agricultural and foreign exchange markets are good examples of perfect competition. The internet has also made the concept of perfect competition somewhat less out of reach, as it has lowered barriers to entry and made comparing prices of similar products much easier.

EVERYDAY EXAMPLE

A typical Saturday morning at your local farmers' market comes close to an example of perfect competition. At local farmers' markets, fresh fruits and vegetables being sold by vendors are virtually identical in quality, and in order to make sales, prices are very similar or identical.

IMPERFECT COMPETITION

Imperfect competition is an umbrella term that covers situations outside of the perfect competition model. It is what we're accustomed to experiencing in North American society. Characteristics of imperfect competition include:

- Differentiation of goods and services help customers distinguish one product from the next
- Buyers develop preferences for brands
- Buyers are willing to spend more for their favorite brands
- Sellers have the ability to demand higher prices

Imperfect competition includes monopoly, monopolistic competition, and oligopoly.

MONOPOLY

A **monopoly** exists when one company dominates the market. Characteristics of monopolies include:

- There are high barriers to entry, such as high capital requirements, technology, or government regulations
- The lack of competition allows sellers to charge high prices
- There are fewer choices available to buyers: a pure monopoly exists when there are no substitutes

The government allows some monopolies to exist to provide public goods, like the postal service, public roads, utilities, and public transportation. In the United States, the U.S. Postal Service is an example of a government monopoly. In some industries, like pharmaceuticals, monopolies exist while new drugs are under patent. **Economies of scale**—cost advantages some large corporations have because of their size—are barriers to entry that prevent some firms from entering a market dominated by a large company.

MONOPOLISTIC COMPETITION

Monopolistic competition includes characteristics of monopolies and competitive markets. Monopolistic competition has the following features:

- The barriers to entry are lower than with monopolies
- Many firms produce and offer similar products and services, though they are not perfect substitutes
- Product differentiation allows companies to gain market advantage
- Marketing and advertising help differentiate products

Examples of monopolistic competition include hotel chains, fast food restaurants, and athletic footwear and apparel brands like Adidas and Nike.

OLIGOPOLY

Oligopolies exist when a small number of firms dominate an industry. Oligopolies have the following characteristics:

- There are barriers to entry that make it difficult for small start-ups to enter the industry
- There are a small number of firms
- Interdependence exists among the industry's firms
- Non-price competition makes advertising and product quality important

In oligopolies, prices remain relatively moderate because of competition, and if one firm decreases prices, the other firms will typically follow. Because of the small number of firms that dominate the industry, prices in an oligopoly tend to be higher than they would be in markets with perfect competition.

Examples of oligopoly industries in the United States include the automobile industry, smartphone operating systems dominated by Apple and Android, and cereal manufacturers such as Kellogg, Post, and General Mills.

Firms in an oligopoly can collude and conspire to fix prices or set output in
order to maximize profits. **Price fixing** occurs when one competitor sets prices
and others follow. A cartel is created when a formal agreement is made between
competing firms to manipulate price and production.

Antitrust laws prohibit collusion in the United States where price fixing is
illegal. Price leadership, on the other hand, is legal. **Price leadership** occurs when
a dominant firm in the market publishes a price and the remaining firms match
that price.

THE OPEC CARTEL

OPEC, the Organization of the Petroleum Exporting Countries, is probably one of the
world's most recognized cartels. The cartel, which was founded in 1960 to coordinate oil
production policies, includes fourteen of the world's major oil-exporting nations.

OPEC lists its mission as "to coordinate and unify the petroleum policies of its
Member Countries and ensure the stabilization of oil markets in order to secure an
efficient, economic and regular supply of petroleum to consumers . . . and a steady
income to producers."

In 1973, OPEC members declared an oil embargo and reduced their production of oil.
By March 1974, when the embargo ended, oil prices had increased by almost 300 percent.
Because OPEC members hold almost 75 percent of crude oil reserves, the cartel has
historically had a huge influence on the market. But in the United States, fracking—a
somewhat controversial process that extracts oil and natural gas from underground—
has affected oil prices and loosened OPEC's hold on the market. In response to this,
worldwide oil production has increased and prices have decreased.

When an airline announces a discounted rate to a destination and other airlines immediately drop their rates to the same destination, the industry has displayed price leadership.

FRANÇOIS QUESNAY
(1694–1774)

Economist and leader in the physiocrat movement François Quesnay was born in 1694 in the north central French village of Méré to a family of small landowners. Quesnay was largely self-taught until 1711, when he began studying medicine and surgery in Paris.

Photo 12/Contributor/Getty

After completing his studies at the community of surgeons of Paris, Quesnay was later awarded a doctor of medicine degree. A few years later, he became the physician of Madame de Pompadour, King Louis XV's most famous mistress.

His interest in economics began in 1756 when he was asked to write an article on farming for an encyclopedia. Quesnay opposed the existing mercantilist movement of his day that supported government intervention to stabilize economies.

In *Tableau Économique*, Quesnay espoused the idea of laissez-faire, or hands-off, government that would allow an economy to find its natural order and called for the government of France to reduce taxes and eliminate trade barriers.

In the United States, antitrust laws explicitly prohibit unlawful mergers and business practices with the stated purpose of upholding competition to benefit consumers. But even with antitrust laws, companies have run afoul of the rules. AT&T, Kodak, and, most recently, tech giants Google, Amazon, and Facebook, have all been accused of manipulating the market to get rid of competition.

So far, we've seen the factors of productions firms use to create goods, and we've examined the various structures companies take to produce these goods. Now let's take a look at the tools economists use to analyze how businesses make decisions about what and how much of a good or service to produce.

> ## "Capitalism is the astounding belief that the most wickedest of men will do the most wickedest of things for the greatest good of everyone."
>
> *—John Maynard Keynes*

CHAPTER 4:
THE PRODUCTION POSSIBILITIES CURVE

Economists look to charts and models to help analyze behavior, determine optimal production points, and create policy. One tool they use is the production possibilities frontier or the **production possibilities curve** (PPC). The production possibilities curve shows the combinations of output that will occur when two goods are produced that use the same set of resources.

The PPC demonstrates a number of concepts:

- Scarcity—finite and limited resources
- Efficiency—optimal allocation of resources
- Diminishing return—the decreasing amount of additional output from each additional unit of input
- Opportunity cost—the forfeited potential gain from choosing one option over another
- Gains of trade—benefits gained from buying and selling goods and services

In a free economy, one of the most important decisions a business makes is what to produce (using the four factors of production) and what combinations of production maximize profits. To show how a firm goes about making that decision, I'll use a small, simple make-believe business called T&K Bakery as an example.

Tamika Brown and her husband Khalil run a small-town bakery. Khalil is an IT consultant who in addition to having his own clients manages the T&K Bakery site. He helps out at the bakery on Saturdays, but because of his limited availability, T&K Bakery also has two employees (labor factor of production): one who serves customers and runs the cash register and one who helps Tamika with the baking. The bakery makes just two products (I told you this was a simple business): chocolate cupcakes and chocolate chip cookies.

T&K Bakery uses a shared rental space as their storefront (land factor of production) and only has access to it from 6 a.m. to 2 p.m. Monday through Saturday (scarce resource). Their other factors of production include their oven, a single electric stand mixer, various baking ingredients, and a few dozen cupcake tins and baking sheets.

Because all of the Browns' resources are limited, Tamika must decide each morning what combination of cookies and cupcakes to produce to meet customer demand and maximize profit. She does that by creating a **production possibilities table**. (Tamika's a bit of a nerd.) The production possibilities table presents the data that will be used to create the production possibilities curve.

Production Possibilities Table

T & K BAKERY		
	# OF CUPCAKES	# OF COOKIES
A	0	100
B	40	80
C	60	60
D	70	40
E	80	0

This table shows us that if Tamika makes 100 cookies a day, she can't bake any cupcakes. But, if she only makes 80 cookies, she can make 40 cupcakes. If she again reduces her daily cookie production to 60, she can make 60 cupcakes.

Here's the production possibilities curve we can create from the chart.

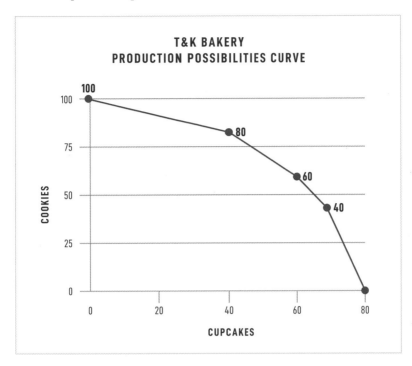

Like the table, the curve shows us that if Tamika dedicates all her resources to baking 80 cupcakes, she can't bake any cookies; if she only bakes 40 cupcakes, she can bake 80 cookies. She can bake any combination of cookies and cupcakes on, above, or beneath the curve, but the points along the curved line represent the bakery's optimal allocation of existing resources for producing both cookies and cupcakes.

Let's take a deeper look at what the curve can tell Tamika about her production possibilities.

The **opportunity cost** of producing something is the value of the thing you're unable to produce: to bake more cupcakes, Tamika will have to bake fewer cookies. In this case, the opportunity cost of increasing cupcake production from 40 to 60 is the 20 fewer cookies Tamika will be able to bake. The slope of the curve indicates the ratio between Tamika's production loss of one product and gain of the other, or the **marginal cost**.

The bowed or concave curve demonstrates the effect of **diminishing returns**—the decreasing benefit Tamika receives from baking additional cupcakes.

So now it's clear that movement along the curve demonstrates efficient combinations of production given the resources Tamika has at a given time. But what happens if T&K Bakery isn't producing its goods efficiently?

In the following graph, the red curved line demonstrates the scenario when T&K Bakery is producing inefficiently. For example, on the red curve, when Tamika is baking 40 cupcakes, she's only making 60 cookies. But, we've already seen that given the bakery's current factors of production, Tamika can produce 80 cookies and 40 cupcakes a day, *when the bakery is operating at optimal production*. If they're only producing 60 cookies when they're making 40 cupcakes, they're losing production and missing out on profits as well.

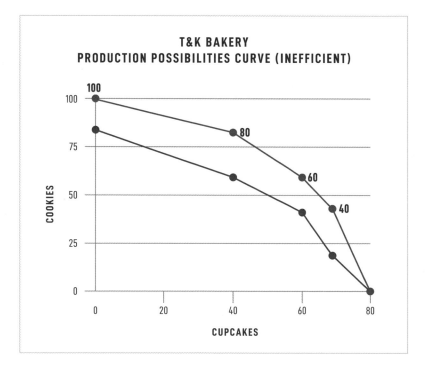

Let's take a look at another scenario. Khalil has snagged a great bargain on a second stand mixer on eBay. With the new mixer (technology), Tamika can increase her production of cookies *and* cupcakes and is now able to bake 160 cookies and 80 cupcakes, operating at a point outside of the original blue curved line. This shift outward is represented by the green curve in the graph below.

T&K BAKERY INCREASED PRODUCTION		
	# OF CUPCAKES	# OF COOKIES
A	0	200
B	80	160
C	120	120
D	140	80
E	160	0

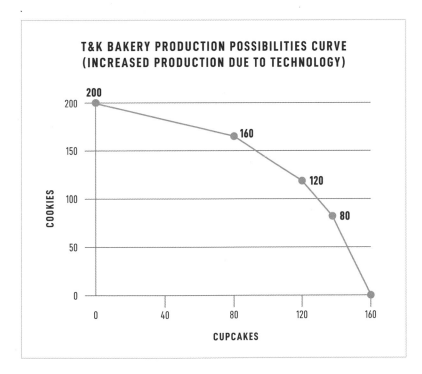

In the real world, making decisions about production is much more complex and includes many additional factors, one being consumer demand. In market economies, firms must not only understand how to efficiently utilize factors of production to create goods and services, but they also have to accurately measure and understand consumer demand, supply, and other aspects of the market.

"For the vast majority of world history, human life–both culture and biology–was shaped by scarcity."

–Martha Beck

JOHN STUART MILL
(1806–1873)

English economist, philosopher, and utilitarian John Stuart Mill was born in Pentonville, London, in 1806 to a strict disciplinarian father who taught him Greek at age three and Latin and geometry by eight years old. He was introduced to the works of Adam Smith as a teenager.

Everett Collection/Shutterstock

Mill's *Principles of Political Economy*, which combined principles of philosophy and economics, helped develop the ideas of opportunity costs, comparative advantage, and economies of scale. Mill believed that personal freedom would increase utility for the entire society and was a strong supporter of free speech and thought. Mill wasn't a big proponent of laissez-faire theory, believing that property rights were not a part of freedom.

Mill was controversial for using his philosophical and social beliefs in his political decision making, including his views about women and enslaved people.

THE ECONOMIC DYNAMIC DUO:
MICROECONOMICS AND MACROECONOMICS

CHAPTER 5

DEMAND

Supply and demand are at the root of every market transaction. The easiest way to think of supply and demand is that supply is the amount of something made available and demand is the amount of it that people want and are willing to pay for. This duo, like Hall and Oates, Batman and Robin, and Chloe and Halle, are inseparable.

Why is the relationship between supply and demand so important? Because it helps us understand how resources are allocated and prices set. It can explain why the prices of airline tickets increase around the holidays, why truffles can cost as much as $168 per ounce, and why gas prices increase after hurricanes. The law of supply and demand explains the relationship between buyers and sellers in a market transaction in a system where scarcity exists.

For the examples that follow, unless otherwise stated, price is the variable and all other things are being held equal.

"People don't know what they want until you show it to them."
—Steve Jobs

Economists make a distinction between demand and quantity demanded. **Demand** refers to a consumer's desire for a good and their willingness to purchase it, while **quantity demanded** refers to how much of a good consumers demand at a certain price point.

The price of an item is usually the most important thing that affects demand, but there are several other factors, known as **demand shifters** or **determinants of demand**, that also play a role. Let's take a look at those.

– WHAT DRIVES DEMAND? –

INCOME

As our **income** increases or decreases, our demand for most products and services usually shifts. If you've always yearned for a luxury vehicle, the promotion you receive at the end of the year may allow you to finally make that purchase and donate your twenty-year-old beater to a good cause. As consumer income rises, overall consumption does too, meaning people buy more of the things they already typically purchase. They might go out to dinner more often or add a scone to their daily coffee shop latte order. The reverse is also true; as consumer income falls, so does consumption, and that one-a-day latte habit might morph into a once-weekly treat.

PERSONAL TASTES AND PREFERENCES

Individual and collective **preferences** shape almost all market decisions. I'm not certain at what point in the 1980s huge bell-bottoms and tie-dye shirts fell out of favor, but at some point, they fell out of fashion and designers stopped making them. Culture, advertising, and the depletion or availability of resources all factor into changing consumer tastes, and they all affect demand. Personal tastes and preferences are probably the hardest to pin down category of demand influencers, but they play a large role in the type and quantity of goods consumers purchase, and companies spend millions of dollars each year to try to understand and influence them. We'll spend more time analyzing this later when we talk about consumer theory.

COMPLEMENTARY GOODS

Certain goods that are usually used together—milk and cereal, hot dogs and hot dog rolls—are known as **complementary goods**, and the price of one of those items affects the demand for the other.

EVERYDAY EXAMPLE

You're in the grocery store doing your weekly shopping on a tight budget and marvel at the high prices of fresh vegetables. But as you peruse the produce aisles, you notice that the supermarket is having a blowout sale on Brussels sprouts, making them, by far, the cheapest fresh vegetables in the produce section. But there's a problem: you hate Brussels sprouts, and even though at these prices the supermarket is practically giving them away, you wouldn't touch them with a ten-foot pole. In this case, your personal preference overrides your demand for low-priced fresh vegetables.

AVAILABILITY OF SUBSTITUTE PRODUCTS

If you're not the kind of customer who's loyal to a particular brand, you'll be open to buying a **substitute product** to save money or if it's more convenient to do so. For example, if a gas station doesn't carry the brand of gum you typically buy, but you want gum and you're in a hurry and already at the gas station, you'll purchase whatever brand is available and located near the register.

ANTICIPATED PRICE

Consumers looking to take advantage of events such as Black Friday and Cyber Monday, for example, will hold off on making purchases, anticipating lower prices on the items they want. When consumers think the price of a product will go up in the future, current demand for that product will increase. If consumers think the price of a product will decline in the future, they will tend to wait to make purchases in the future when the prices fall.

PRICE

As I mentioned above, all other things being equal, **price** usually has the biggest effect on demand, typically exhibiting an inverse correlation. In other words, as prices for goods rise, the quantity demanded for those goods will decrease. This principle is known as the law of demand.

– LAW OF DEMAND –

The **law of demand** states that as the price of an item increases, the quantity demanded of that item will decrease, and if the price increases, the quantity demanded will decrease. There are exceptions to this, which we'll discuss later, but for most goods and services, this law holds, and it makes sense, right? The more expensive an item gets, the less of that item most consumers are willing and able to purchase.

A **demand schedule** is a table that illustrates the relationship between price and quantity demanded. Let's check back in with T&K Bakery to see what a demand schedule for their cupcakes would look like.

T&K BAKERY DAILY CUPCAKE SALES DEMAND SCHEDULE		
SCENARIO	QUANTITY DEMANDED	PRICE IN $
A	75	2.5
B	40	2.75
C	20	3.5
D	10	5

This demand schedule tells us that if Tamika priced her cupcakes at $2.50 each, her customers would demand 75 cupcakes a day, and if she doubled that price to $5.00 per cupcake, the quantity of cupcakes demanded daily would drop to 10. The table highlights the inverse relationship between price and quantity demanded. The relationship between the quantity demanded of a good and a change in its price is known as **price elasticity of demand**.

QUICK TIP

Price Elasticity of Demand = % Change in Quantity Demanded / % Change in Price

A demand curve is created from a demand schedule and illustrates this inverse relationship. When we create the curve for T&K Bakery's demand schedule, it looks like this.

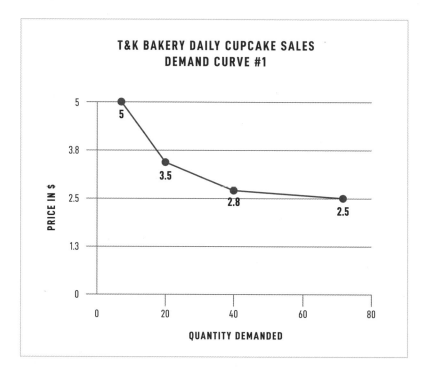

This demand curve provides us with a lot of useful information. For one, the downward slope demonstrates the inverse relationship between price and quantity demanded—again, this means that as prices fall, Tamika's customers demand more cupcakes. It also shows us the demand at each price along the curve. So, at a price of $2.75, Tamika's customers would demand 40 cupcakes.

The curve's slope tells us how sensitive customers are to price changes. In this case, the demand for T&K Bakery cupcakes falls sharply in response to price increases. The degree to which the quantity demanded changes when the price changes is known as **elasticity of demand** or **demand elasticity**. The relatively flat curve shown here indicates that Tamika's customers' demand for cupcakes is highly elastic and that they react strongly to price increases.

Customers can be sensitive to price drops as well. Remember our Brussels sprouts example from earlier where your personal tastes precluded you from purchasing the cruciferous vegetable? What if you had a change of heart and

ALFRED MARSHALL
(1842–1924)

Alfred Marshall was born to a middle-class family in London, England. Marshall was educated at Merchant Taylors' School and at St. Johns College in Cambridge and later became a professor of political economy at the University of Cambridge.

Historic Collection/Alamy Stock Photo

Marshall's *Principles of Economics* (1890) is considered his seminal contribution to the field of economics. In it, he introduced a number of new concepts, including consumer surplus—the difference between the price someone pays for a good and what they would be willing to pay rather than going without it. Marshall wrote that the price and output of goods were determined by both their supply and demand. He also introduced the concept of buyers' sensitivity to price: the price elasticity of demand.

Additional works by Marshall include *Industry and Trade* (1919), which studied industrial organization, and *Money, Credit, and Commerce* (1923), which, among other subjects, included his plan for using silver and gold as the monetary base.

Marshall was one of the foremost voices in British economics from 1890 until his death in 1924 and is considered one of the founders of the neoclassical school of economics.

QUICK TIP

Changes in price move along the demand curve and are associated with a particular point on the curve. Changes in other factors shift the curve to the left or right.

decided to give Brussels sprouts one last try? You hightail it from the seafood department back to produce, but by the time you make it back there, the sprouts are all sold out. The Brussels sprouts were a highly elastic product, one that was very sensitive to a drop in price.

So, what would a demand schedule and curve look like if the demand for a product were less elastic? Let's visit the bakery again.

T&K BAKERY DAILY CUPCAKE SALES		
SCENARIO	QUANTITY DEMANDED	PRICE IN $
A	75	2.5
B	70	2.75
C	65	3.5
D	55	5

In this alternate demand schedule, when cupcake prices increase, the quantity demanded still decreases, but at a much lower rate. The steep demand curve illustrates the relative inelasticity of the quantity demanded relative to price.

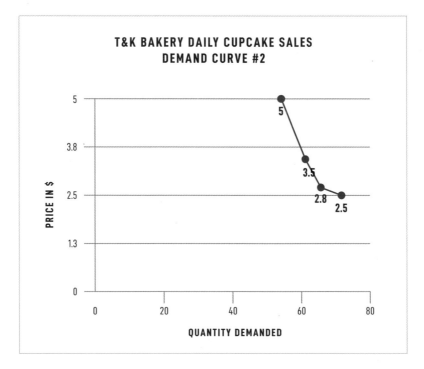

When the quantity demanded of a good doesn't change as the price changes, the demand for that good is said to be **inelastic**.

Low elasticity or inelasticity indicates that consumers buy the product regardless of changes to price or other external factors. We're all familiar with products with inelastic demand. Grocery staples like milk, bread, and chicken, and items such as toilet paper, underwear, and shoes, typically have low elasticity.

The demand for prescription drugs, cigarettes, and alcohol tend to be inelastic, because price rarely affects our demand for those goods. Portable fans on hot summer days and mittens in the winter are examples of products whose demand can be inelastic depending on the time of year.

Gasoline is another example of a product with a typically low elasticity of demand. Workers who rely on their vehicles to get to work can't be highly sensitive to changes in gas prices because telling their bosses they can't come to work because gas prices went up is a surefire way to end up out of a job. But high gas prices in the summer, however, can curtail people's willingness and ability to take road trips, resulting in staycations.

High elasticity of demand, on the other hand, exists when consumers adjust their buying habits as a result of price increases. These nonessential goods like jewelry, eating out, and certain electronics are often cut from a household budget when prices increase or income decreases.

HOW NON-PRICE FACTORS AFFECT QUANTITY DEMANDED

Non-price factors include changes in consumer income and shifts in tastes and preferences. Let's say that, unfortunately for T&K Bakery and the chocolate-loving world, a new study is released that shows that chocolate contains a formerly unknown allergen that causes severe itching among most people. Despite the few die-hard chocolate lovers who will probably risk it anyway, the overall demand for chocolate products, including chocolate cupcakes, will decrease. This decreased demand will result in fewer cupcake sales at every price point.

NORMAL, LUXURY, AND INFERIOR GOODS

As we learned earlier, a change in income is a non-price factor that affects the demand for most goods. When income increases, the demand for normal goods increases; when income drops, demand does as well. The demand for normal goods and income are positively correlated, and this relationship is known as the **income elasticity of demand** (YED).

Normal goods are goods that experience increased demand when income increases. **Necessity goods** are a type of normal good for which the income elasticity of demand is between zero and one. Necessity goods include most food items, housing, electricity, and cigarettes.

Luxury goods are a type of normal good that has an income elasticity of demand greater than one. Increases in income result in a larger increase in demand for these goods. Luxury automobiles (it's right there in the name) and high-end jewelry are examples of luxury goods.

Inferior goods are goods that have a negative income elasticity of demand. Consumers buy fewer inferior goods when their incomes increase. Examples of inferior goods are off-brand food items, canned meats, and in some scenarios, public transportation.

FORMULA

Income elasticity of demand = % change in quantity demanded / % change in income. Another way to write this formula is (New Quantity Demand − Old Quantity Demand) / (Old Quantity Demand) / (New Income − Old Income) / (Old Income)

EVERYDAY EXAMPLE

After five years in the cubicle war trenches, Maria's promotion has finally come through. In her first post-raise trip to the grocery store, she bypasses the store-brand coffee and buys the specialty brand her nemesis is always carrying on about. In this scenario, the store-brand coffee is the inferior good.

STATUS SYMBOLS AND VEBLEN GOODS

Rolex, Louis Vuitton, and Bentley are all examples of Veblen goods. **Veblen goods** are those for which demand increases as price increases. Veblens are sometimes referred to as "snob goods" and differ from some luxury items because higher prices make them even more desirable. Veblen goods defy the downward-sloping demand curve associated with the law of demand, demonstrating upward-sloping demand curves instead.

Why does this happen? Veblen products are status symbols: objects that signify high social ranking and wealth. These products are marketed based on their exclusivity and the fact that they are out of reach to the average consumer. They carry very strong brand identity, so much so that even the logoed shopping bags of these items are status symbols.

Veblen goods aren't relegated to big-ticket tangible goods. Exclusive club memberships and services from celebrity makeup artists and hair stylists are also examples of Veblen goods.

"Living in the lap of luxury isn't bad except that you never know when luxury is going to stand up."

—Orson Welles

Elasticity of demand factors into how firms conduct business. Retail stores plan their sales schedules well in advance. They often won't announce sales too far in advance, though, hoping to prevent customers from curtailing their regular shopping, because when consumers know a sale is around the corner, they tend to stop buying in anticipation of lower prices. On the other hand, during a sale, a retailer will typically publish when discount prices will end to drive consumers to buy more of a product before high prices return.

With a highly elastic product, this sales model will prove effective. With an inelastic or "low elasticity" product, it will not. Consumers will continue to buy in steady numbers regardless of how they think future prices will move. Whether products are elastic or inelastic, firms must know how much to produce at any given time at a given price, and these decisions are based on the law of supply.

DID YOU KNOW?

The most expensive Gucci item ever sold was the Gucci Stuart Hues belt, which went for $250,000.

CHAPTER 6:

SUPPLY

In a market economy, firms require payment to supply goods and services, and the more of these goods and services the public demands, the more expensive it becomes for firms to produce them.

— THE LAW OF SUPPLY —

The **law of supply** states that as prices rise, the quantity supplied of a good also rises. And the inverse is also true: when price decreases, the quantity supplied also decreases. In other words, higher prices induce businesses to increase the quantity of goods they supply because higher prices will lead to higher profits. An example of this would be banks offering more loans when interest rates rise.

The **supply schedule** is a table that shows the relationship between price and quantity supplied. Let's visit another small-town business. This one is called Simon Sews and its owner, Simon, creates baubles and bedazzled items for online sale. He's considering dedicating some of his resources (factors of production) to making cloth face masks for sale on his online shop.

SIMON SEWS SUPPLY SCHEDULE	
QUANTITY SUPPLIED	PRICE PER MASK IN $
2	4
10	5
20	8
30	10
40	12
50	15

This supply schedule shows the minimum prices Simon will accept to produce certain quantities of masks each week. For example, at a price of $5 per mask, Simon is willing to supply 10 masks. His decision to do so is based on the benefit he would gain from giving up resources to make those masks. These aren't the prices Simon *wants* for his masks; if he had his way, he'd charge at least $20 per mask no matter how many he made, especially for the bedazzled ones. No, these prices represent the minimum a buyer could pay Simon to produce masks at the quantities shown.

Simon Sews' supply curve looks like this:

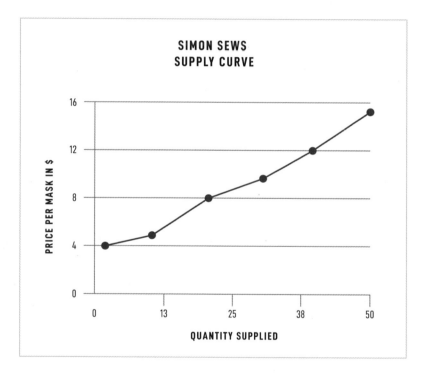

The supply curve slopes upward because when Simon expects to receive higher prices, he'll produce more masks. Movement along the curve represents variations in pricing. For example, at a price point of $6, indicated by the red dot in the following chart, Simon is willing to produce 15 masks.

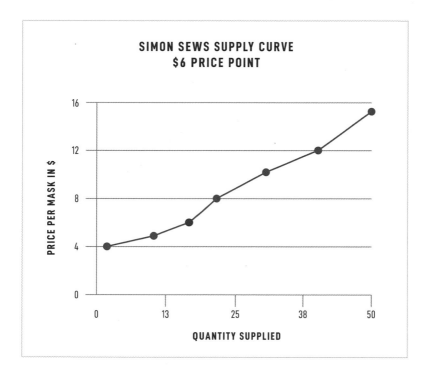

SIMON SEWS SUPPLY CURVE
$6 PRICE POINT

If Simon can get $8 per mask, he'll produce 20 masks. And if buyers were willing to pay $15 per mask, Simon's sewing machine pedals would be hot to the touch as he worked to produce 50 masks. But if Simon could only get $5 per mask, he'd only produce 10 masks. And if a buyer offered Simon $1 per mask, after a few choice words, Simon would quit the mask-making business and return to his first love: bedazzling baseball caps.

What happens if something other than price changes in our Simon Sews scenario?

– FACTORS OTHER THAN PRICE –
THAT AFFECT THE SUPPLY CURVE

Production costs determine the slope and location of a producer's supply curve. If Simon's production costs increase, customers have to pay him more to produce the same quantity of masks. In this example, let's say the cost of the elastic used in making masks almost doubles. Now, the minimum price Simon will accept for producing 20 masks has increased from $8 to $12 per mask. The new supply curve looks like this:

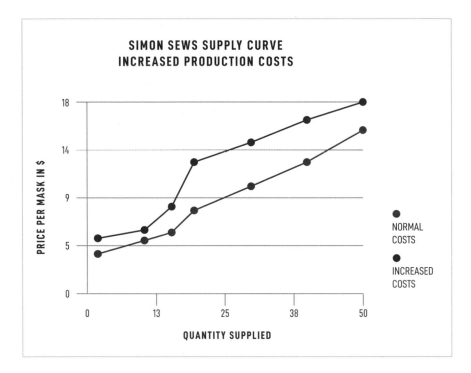

The new supply curve shifts upward to indicate the higher minimum price required at each quantity of production. Several factors can contribute to a change in production costs that shifts the supply curve. These include:

- Changes in worker productivity
- Tax increases or decreases
- Improved technology
- Investment in capital

Let's have a look at how changes in some of these other factors would affect Simon.

One evening while browsing through his online neighborhood yard sale exchange, Simon spots a coveted Sew-Baby 5000, the mother of all sewing machines. The Sew-Baby 5000 practically threads itself, and the person offering the Sew-Baby is throwing in a hot-fix rhinestone bedazzler to boot. When Simon collects himself, he contacts the seller, and twenty-four hours later, he's the proud owner of a good-as-new Sew-Baby 5000.

With his new machine, Simon uses less thread and material to make each mask and significantly reduces his sewing time, changes that reduce Simon's overall cost of production.

SELF TEST

How will Simon's new sewing machine affect Simon Sews' supply curve?
Answer: Technological advances shift the supply curve to the right.

– INTERSECTING SUPPLY AND DEMAND – CURVES: MARKET EQUILIBRIUM

Theoretically, when a market price is too low, buyers demand more of a good than suppliers are willing to offer. In this scenario, supply and demand are out of balance, resulting in market disequilibrium. On the shelves, this looks like your favorite items frequently being out of stock. When that happens, market prices will begin to rise until they're at a point where the quantity demanded is equal to the quantity supplied. The point where the supply and demand curves cross is known as the **equilibrium price**. At the market equilibrium point, supply and demand are balanced and prices are stable.

Let's look at what market equilibrium looks like for Simon Sews.

SIMON SEWS MARKET EQUILIBRIUM		
QUANTITY SUPPLIED	QUANTITY DEMANDED	PRICE PER MASK IN $
2	50	4
10	40	5
20	20	8
30	10	10
40	5	12
50	2	15

At the price point of $8, indicated in the graph by the point where the demand and supply curve intersect, buyers demand 20 masks and Simon is willing to provide 20 masks.

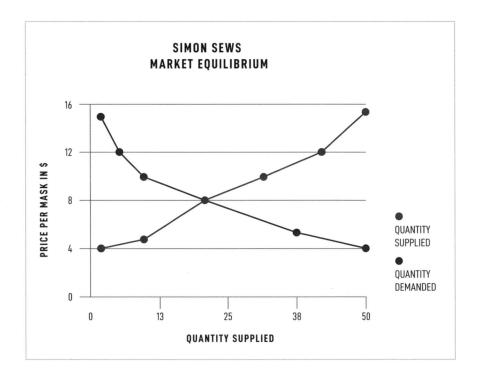

In microeconomics, equilibrium represents the supply and demand of a product. In macroeconomics, it refers to supply and demand of the society as a whole.

Any price besides the market price—the price where the two curves intersect—provides incentive for buyers and sellers to move toward equilibrium. When there is **excess supply**, or surplus, the quantity demanded by buyers is less than the quantity supplied by sellers. In response, suppliers will reduce inventory by having a sale. Overstock.com and Big Lots are companies that sell items at reduced prices so that producers can reduce inventory. Suppliers will keep reducing the price until it falls to the equilibrium price.

Excess demand occurs when buyers want more of a product than suppliers have available to sell. In this scenario, there is a shortage of products. Toilet paper, hand sanitizer, and face shields were all items that were in excess demand during the COVID-19 pandemic, for example.

In our theoretical models, price adjusts in response to supply and demand until equilibrium is established. But what happens when this doesn't occur naturally? In these situations, the government in a mixed economic system will step in to institute controls. **Price controls** are legally imposed price minimums or maximums for certain goods. **Price floors** help keep the price of a product *above* equilibrium value, while **price ceilings** keep product prices *below* equilibrium.

Remember the essential goods I mentioned earlier? The government controls prices on certain essential goods, setting ceilings to aid with affordability. One of the most recognizable examples of a government-established price floor is the minimum wage. The **minimum wage** sets legal hourly wage minimums for employees. Another form of government price control is farm subsidies that add incentives for farmers to use land to produce some products and not others.

Rent control in New York City is an example of a price ceiling that was intended to ensure affordable housing in certain areas of the city. Instead, rent control actually reduced the overall supply of rental space and ended up contributing to higher prices in the overall market. Critics of price controls point out that in a free market, government-imposed prices can lead to excess demand and supply.

THE MINIMUM WAGE
AND THE COST OF LABOR

The availability of workers, and what they are paid, is a factor of production that affects a firm's overall costs. Profit-seeking firms attempt to reduce costs in all areas of production. Historically, this has meant workers being paid less than a living wage, children working when they should be in school, and unsafe, poorly regulated work environments.

In 1938, The U.S. Congress passed the Fair Labor Standards Act (FLSA). The FLSA outlined guidelines for child labor, employment status, overtime, and minimum wage. The federal minimum wage is a type of price control enacted by the government that establishes a minimum required pay (price of labor for producers) for U.S. workers employed by companies with revenues of at least $500,000 or those working in places such as government agencies, hospitals, nursing homes, and schools.

The federal minimum wage was enacted to help stabilize the post-depression economy and to protect employees by establishing a minimum standard of living. Congress created the Wage-Hour Division of the Department of Labor to oversee and enforce minimum wage requirements. Along with the division, the secretary of labor holds the authority to request employer records and sue to recover unpaid benefits on behalf of employees.

The current federal wage became effective on July 24, 2009, and is $7.25 per hour. Since the wage was set in 1938, legislation has increased the rate a total of nine times.

THOMAS AQUINAS
(1225–1274)

Thomas Aquinas was an Italian philosopher and theologian born in Roccasecca, Sicily, to parents who owned a feudal domain.

He began attending the University of Naples in 1239, and after secretly joining an order of Dominican monks, was kidnapped by his family and held captive for a year as they tried to change his religious views. When he was granted his freedom a year later, Aquinas continued his studies in Naples, Paris, and Cologne, Germany, where he was ordained in 1250.

CkyBe/Shutterstock

Aquinas is considered one of the Catholic Church's greatest theologians. His unfinished but influential *Summa Theologica* argued the case for approaching economics from the lens of moral virtue.

Thomas Aquinas condemned usury, the practice of making loans at high, unethical interest rates. He reasoned that doing so was, in a sense, receiving income for nothing, and he believed that money should not be used to generate even more money. In *Summa Theologica*, Aquinas posited that people who took out loans did so only because they desperately needed the money, but that lenders had more resources and therefore did not need the interest they would be receiving from the loan. He argued that the practice was wrong and detrimental to society.

Aquinas also felt it was immoral for suppliers to raise prices based on local conditions and believed that profit should be realized based on the producer's labor and not based on the buyer's need. Aquinas is most widely known for advancing the theory of just price *(Justum Pretium)*—the belief that equality and fairness should be present in economic transactions.

CHAPTER 7

CONSUMER THEORY

O ne of the things everyone reading this book has in common is that we are all consumers. Regardless of where we're from and where we live, we pay for and consume goods and services. The World Bank reported that in 2018, worldwide consumption expenditure was $63.083 trillion (USD). Humans consume a lot of stuff.

As we've already begun to see, the field of economics isn't just concerned with tables and curves. Understanding what guides consumer behavior is also an important part of the field, because understanding behavior can help individuals, firms, and governments become more efficient.

There are obvious challenges involved with trying to understand and predict consumer behavior. For one, much of economic thought hinges on the assumption that consumers make rational choices based on having complete information. This **rational choice theory** assumes that in situations of scarcity, individuals always act in their own self-interest, choosing the option that maximizes their satisfaction and well-being. The theory asserts that these choices also benefit the economy as a whole.

But in the real world, few things are constant, neither firms nor individuals always have access to full information, and consumers don't always behave rationally. And even when they do behave rationally (or try to), people are forced to make choices because of scarcity—scarcity of time, income, resources, and opportunity—that sometimes don't pay off. Despite this, or perhaps because of it, it's important to try to understand how various factors shape our decisions.

Consumer theory is a branch of microeconomics that studies consumer behavior—how and why individuals spend their money. Studying consumer behavior helps economists understand how spending affects individual households, firms, and the economy as a whole.

– UTILITY –

Utility refers to the satisfaction received from consuming a good. The **total utility** is a measurement of the total satisfaction received from consuming a good. As a good is consumed, the total utility received from consuming it increases. **Marginal utility** refers to the incremental increase in utility received from consuming an additional unit of a good. A **util** is a unit of measurement of satisfaction.

DID YOU KNOW?

Fast food giant McDonald's created broccoli that tasted like bubble gum.
Spoiler alert: It wasn't a hit with kids.

EVERYDAY EXAMPLE

It's a Friday night after a long workweek, and the only thing you've been thinking about is diving into the box of candy you've been saving all week. The first piece of candy is amazing as it melts in your mouth, and the satisfaction you receive from consuming it—the *utility*—is high. The second and third pieces have much the same effect, and your satisfaction, or *total utility*, is still increasing. By the fourth piece, however, you notice the candy isn't quite as amazing as it was when you first started, and by the sixth piece, you're questioning your life choices and chasing the candy with a bottle of wine. You're now experiencing *diminishing marginal utility*.

CONSUMER BUYING BEHAVIOR

Whether we're shopping for shirts or shampoo, donuts or diamonds, our buying behavior typically falls into one of the following categories.

EXTENDED DECISION-MAKING

If you've ever been in the market for a new car or home, you've likely experienced the extended decision-making process. Maybe you pored over consumer ratings reports and spent weeks or months agonizing over your decision. Totally understandable, and expected when making a high-involvement, high-value purchase of a good you purchase infrequently.

LIMITED DECISION-MAKING

Products that you purchase more frequently and are not major financial investments, but are somewhat important to you, fall into the limited decision-making category. These decisions require a moderate amount of research because while buying them won't break the bank, they'll still need to meet your expectations. An example of limited decision-making would be deciding on what brand of jeans or handbag to purchase.

ROUTINE RESPONSE

Your morning latte, your favorite lipstick color, and the aftershave you've bought religiously for the last ten years are all examples of routine response buying behavior. These frequent, low-involvement purchases require very little research and decision-making, so much so that your buying behavior is almost automatic.

IMPULSE BUYING

There's a reason gum, candy, and magazines are usually located near the checkout lane. These impulse buys don't care that you hadn't planned on buying gum or reading the latest gossip on your favorite celebrity. Impulse buys are all about immediate gratification.

The **law of diminishing marginal utility** states that the amount of satisfaction a consumer receives from a good *decreases* as consumption of that good increases. A few pieces of candy is the perfect afternoon snack, but the law of diminishing marginal utility says that each subsequent piece of candy will provide less and less satisfaction. Most goods return diminishing marginal utility, and knowing that helps economists understand buyer behavior.

Let's take a closer look at how utility works by analyzing the gummy bear eating habits of an individual. By now, you shouldn't be surprised to learn there's a table for that.

This table illustrates the utils (units of satisfaction) our candy eater gets from eating each handful of gummy bears.

QUANTITY OF GUMMY BEARS CONSUMED (IN HANDFULS)	UTILS
0	0
1	6
2	10
3	13
4	10
5	8

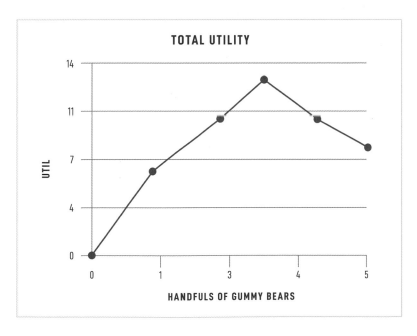

The table below illustrates diminishing marginal utility—as our gummy bear eater consumes increasing handfuls of gummy bears, their total utility increases, but only up to the third handful of gummy bears. Beyond three handfuls, their total utility actually begins to decrease. This is seen in the last column where at four handfuls of gummy bears, marginal utility is negative, and our gummy bear eater is made worse off by eating that handful.

QUANTITY OF GUMMY BEARS CONSUMED (IN HANDFULS)	UTILS	MARGINAL UTILITY
0	0	–
1	6	6
2	10	4
3	13	3
4	10	-3
5	8	-5

In the example above, the gummy bear eater might forgo the third handful of gummy bears and opt for a glass of wine instead. Because of diminishing marginal utility, consumers will often rank items to help them make decisions, keeping in mind their budgets and the prices of the alternatives they're considering. When faced with budget limitations and diminishing utility, consumers try to make decisions that will maximize their utility.

Someone who wants to return to school but whose car needs immediate repairs must rank between paying the $2,000 in car repairs or enrolling in class for the upcoming semester.

The small business owner who is making a profit must choose between reinvesting that money in the business to increase production or using that money to go on a well-needed vacation. This ranking is one of the tools economists use to analyze consumer motivation.

THE GROWING GLOBAL MIDDLE CLASS

The middle class is growing around the world. In 2009, the global middle class numbered 1.8 billion people. By 2020, that number likely increased to 3.2 billion. Asian countries account for the bulk of this growth. Globalization, spurred by technology and the relative ease of flow of goods and services around the world, has resulted in a growth rate that anticipates that by 2030 two-thirds of the world's population will be a part of the global middle class. So how is the burgeoning global middle class spending its money?

According to a 2012 article in *OECD Observer*, the top five expenditure areas for the global middle class ages thirty-five to sixty-four are:

- Housing, fuel, and power
- Transportation
- Food and beverage
- Recreation and culture
- Miscellaneous goods and services

– POVERTY AND CONSUMER CHOICE –

We can't talk about consumer behavior without talking about those whose choices are limited because of poverty. Globally, over 736 million people live in extreme poverty, defined as living on less than $1.90 a day. According to World Vision, approximately 1.3 billion people in 104 low- and middle-income countries (LMIC) live in multidimensional poverty, a measurement that includes lack of access to health care, education, and adequate living conditions.

In the United States, the census uses a set of money income thresholds to determine who is in poverty. Poverty thresholds are dollar amounts that are considered the minimum necessary to meet basic needs and are updated annually by the Census Bureau. The income of all members of a household are used to determine the threshold, and it includes, among other income sources, earnings, unemployment, Social Security, veterans' payments, and alimony and child support. For the sake of establishing the threshold, money income does not include noncash benefits like food stamps, housing subsidies, tax credits, or capital gains or losses.

Poverty guidelines, sometimes referred to as the "federal poverty level" (FPL), are issued by the Department of Health and Human Services (HHS) and are a simplified version of the poverty threshold. These are used to help determine financial eligibility for certain government programs.

In 2020 for a family of four in the forty-eight contiguous states, the poverty guideline was $26,200. Programs that use the guidelines to determine eligibility include Head Start, the Supplemental Nutrition Assistance Program (SNAP), and the Children's Health Insurance Program.

Race, education, age, health, and education levels are all factors that affect the likelihood of living in poverty in the United States. In 2019, the poverty rate was 10.5 percent, or 34 million people in poverty, down 1.3 percentage points from 2018. The poverty rate in the United States has fallen 4.3 percentage points since 2014. In 2018, the following percentages of these groups lived in poverty:

- 10.6 percent of men
- 12.9 percent of women
- 16.2 percent of all children, or one in six
- 25.7 percent of people living with a disability
- 4.7 percent of married couples

The U.S. poverty rates by race, according to Poverty USA, were as follows:

- 25.4 percent of Native Americans
- 20.8 percent of Black Americans
- 17.6 percent of Hispanic Americans
- 10.1 percent of White Americans
- 10.1 percent of Asian Americans

These statistics on poverty are important, not only for the human toll poverty takes on individuals who lack the resources to obtain adequate food, clothing, and shelter, but because they have a larger economic impact as well. When wages are low, communities suffer from lack of education, poor infrastructure, and the inability to build wealth. This not only impacts local communities but also the overall economy. And even those who aren't among the world's poorest can benefit from increased access to affordable housing and education, which have both been proven to strengthen communities.

Around the world, governments and societies are faced with the challenges of managing resources in a way that maximizes satisfaction for its citizens. Macroeconomics is the field of economics that studies the way governments and societies behave, and we'll be taking a look at that in the next chapter.

JOHN LOCKE
(1632–1704)

English philosopher John Locke was born in Somerset, England, in 1632. He is known as the father of political liberalism and his writing and philosophies inspired the European Enlightenment and the U.S. Constitution. Locke's political thought was based on the concept of a social contract between society's citizens.

Everett Collection/Shutterstock

In *Treatises*, Locke put forward the philosophy that labor was the possession of the laborer, and that anything that the labor was applied to was therefore owned by the laborer. In a 1691 letter to Parliament, *Some Considerations on the Consequences of the Lowering of Interest and the Raising of the Value of Money*, Locke referred to supply as quantity and demand as rent, and promoted the theory of supply and demand as regulating price. Locke also wrote about scarcity and the functions of money as a measure of value and the promise for a good.

CHAPTER 8

MACROECONOMICS

> ## "The care of human life and happiness, and not their destruction, is the first and only object of good government."
>
> *—Thomas Jefferson*

W e've spent the last several chapters exploring microeconomic concepts and how they affect individuals and firms. In this section, we'll examine macroeconomics. As a refresher, macroeconomics studies the activities and behaviors of a society as a whole.

Almost every national evening newscast covers macroeconomic concepts that affect our country, though the term **macroeconomics** is rarely used. **Unemployment**, **stimulus checks**, **inflation**, and **recession** are all terms heard frequently on the news, and they are all topics macroeconomics covers. Let's delve into them now, starting with GDP.

– GDP –

The **gross domestic product** (GDP) is a calculation of the value of all goods and services a country produces during a given period of time. In the United States, the Bureau of Labor Statistics (BLS) maintains data that is collected by the Bureau of Economic Analysis (BEA) to compute GDP. GDP doesn't include volunteer work, the work of stay-at-home parents, or illegal activities.

Federal and local governments, the Federal Reserve, and corporations are among those who use GDP and related statistics to make decisions about, among other things, taxes, interest rates, and labor and employment.

The GDP includes four categories: personal consumption expenditures, investment, government spending, and net exports.

Personal Consumption Expenditures	Also called consumer spending: the goods and services people buy, such as groceries, clothing, cellphone service, and health care.
+ Investment	This is business spending on fixed assets such as land, buildings, and equipment, plus investment in unsold inventory; also includes purchases of homes by consumers.
+ Government Spending	Spending by federal, state, and local governments to provide goods and services, such as schools, roads, and national defense.
+ Net Exports	Also known as exports minus imports (X – M): the value of exports to other countries minus the value of imports into the United States. *Why are imports subtracted? Consumers, businesses, and governments spend some of their money on imports. U.S. production would be overstated if the formula didn't remove imports.*
= GDP	The total market value of the goods and services produced within the United States in a year.

GDP FOUR-PART FORMULA

GDP = Personal Consumption Expenditures + Investment + Government Spending + Net Exports

The BEA provides quarterly and annual estimates of the country's GDP. As of 2020, the U.S. GDP was $19 trillion. GDP is often reported as a percentage instead of a dollar figure. During the second quarter of 2020, for example, GDP decreased at an annual rate of 31.4 percent, in large part due to the worldwide pandemic. The rate is based on what's known as the "real GDP," which is the GDP adjusted for inflation.

GDP is important for a number of reasons. First, it provides information about the state of a nation's economy and how it is performing. Increasing real GDP—GDP adjusted for inflation—is typically a sign that an economy is doing well. And when GDP is strong, businesses increase hiring and pay higher wages. In turn, consumers spend more on goods and services.

GDP does not tell us about a country's standard of living and can mask income inequality and general well-being, or hide issues of resource depletion, pollution, and global warming.

PERSONAL CONSUMPTION EXPENDITURES

Personal consumption expenditures account for approximately 70 percent of GDP. Also known as consumer spending, this category includes all the goods and services purchased by individual households. Goods are defined as tangible objects that people purchase and are broken down into nondurable (or consumables) and durable goods.

Nondurable goods have a life span of less than three years and are consumed only once and/or immediately. Food and clothing are examples of nondurable goods.

Durable goods, like personal computers, large appliances, and cars, are not consumed quickly or all at once and tend to last for more than three years.

Services are expenditures where no physical goods are exchanged between the buyer and seller.

INVESTMENT

Business **investments** include the purchase of fixed assets—long-term tangible goods such as machinery and equipment—used to produce consumer goods. Fixed assets also include home purchases by consumers and commercial real estate construction. The BEA does not include home resales in GDP calculations because new buildings are added to the GDP the year they are built.

GOVERNMENT SPENDING

Government spending includes any spending on goods and services at the federal, state, and local level to provide public goods to its citizens, including national defense, education, and health care. Government spending is financed through taxation and borrowing domestically and internationally.

NET EXPORTS

Exports are goods and services that are sold abroad, while imports are goods that are bought in a different country than where they were produced. **Net exports** is the difference between a country's exports and imports. Because the United States imports more goods than it exports, it operates with a trade deficit.

− TRADE −

The exchange and buying and selling of goods and services are part of every market system. A simple example of trade takes place at school lunch tables when a kid, tired of their peanut butter and jelly sandwich, trades it for a turkey and provolone on rye. Another form of trade, which we'll discuss in more detail in a later section, involves buying and selling stocks and securities.

When goods are made in one country and sold in another, this is known as **international trade**.

Trade also allows consumers to buy and consume products that may have otherwise been unavailable in their country. Italian leather, French wine, and cocoa beans from Ghana are all examples of products the United States imports from abroad.

TRADE SURPLUSES AND DEFICITS

When a country's exports exceed its imports, the country is running a **trade surplus**. There are a number of benefits of a trade surplus:

- Additional cash that allows for additional investment
- Job creation
- Decreased government spending
- Increased foreign investment

But there are also downsides to a trade surplus:

- Increased inflation
- Job outsourcing
- A reduction of domestic industries
- Degradation of natural resources

A **trade deficit** occurs when a country's imports exceed its exports. Trade deficits aren't inherently bad. Because trade lowers prices, it can reduce the chances of inflation. Deficits can also improve a country's standard of living by giving individuals access to a wider variety of goods and services. But long-term trade deficits can hurt economic growth and job creation as firms outsource jobs in an effort to become more competitive in the global marketplace.

– ECONOMIC DEVELOPMENT –

Economic development occurs within a given economy when growth results in increased wealth for individuals within the community. This growth occurs when limited resources of land, labor, capital, and entrepreneurship—the four factors of production—are allocated in a way that positively influences things like employment, income, and business activity. Economic development involves intentional effort by government and leaders at the national, regional, or local level to direct investment toward opportunities that can create and sustain growth. Whenever you hear terms such as "industrialization" and "modernization," it's typically within the context of discussing economic development.

Examples of economic development include North America shifting from farming and mining economies to manufacturing in the nineteenth century and the shift to service industries in the twentieth. Government policies that promote economic development include K-12 education programs, affordable housing initiatives, and job creation programs.

Though economic development and community development often go hand in hand, community development differs in that it is focused on making communities better places to live and work. In other words, community development focuses on the quality of life, while economic development is focused on the creation of wealth and income. And as the saying goes, "Money can't buy happiness."

NAFTA

The North American Free Trade Agreement, or NAFTA, is a treaty between the United States, Canada, and Mexico that went into effect on January 1, 1994. The agreement applies to various imports and exports and was created to increase North American trade among the partnering countries. NAFTA:

- Eliminated nontariff barriers between the partnering countries
- Eliminated tariffs on qualifying products and reduced tariffs for auto parts and automobiles
- Toughened industrial, health, and safety standards and improved the speed of export
- Instituted inspections and certifications
- Increased protection of intellectual property rights

NAFTA gave national good status to imports from NAFTA countries, essentially preventing state and local governments from imposing taxes or tariffs on qualifying goods. NAFTA opened Mexican markets to U.S. companies, resulting in lower grocery and fuel prices for consumers. It quadrupled trade between 1993 and 2019, boosting economic growth for its participating countries. It also created jobs across the United States, even on imports from Mexico, because 40 percent of the imports came from American companies.

But some estimates say that NAFTA led to the loss of over 680,000 jobs, largely from manufacturing industries, including automotive and textile industries in California, Texas, Michigan, and New York. This outsourcing of jobs led to lower wages in certain industries in these states.

NAFTA didn't only affect American jobs. Agricultural products subsidized by the U.S. government resulted in Mexican farmers going out of business. Some of these farmers eventually crossed the Mexican border into the United States looking for work.

In July 2020, the US-Mexico-Canada Agreement (USMCA) officially replaced NAFTA. The new agreement fulfilled a promise made by President Donald Trump during his 2016 campaign. The USMCA is similar to NAFTA with some notable changes. These changes include increasing the requirement that vehicle parts be made in one of the three member countries from 62.5 percent to 75 percent. The USMCA also established a wage floor of $16 an hour for labor involved in making some vehicle parts.

The new agreement was estimated to create 176,000 jobs after six years and increase GDP by 0.35 percent. The change is being called modest by the U.S. International Trade Commission.

— THE BUSINESS CYCLE —

The **business cycle**, also known as the **trade cycle** or **boom and bust cycle**, refers to fluctuations in GDP over time. Cycles occur when economies "overheat" during a period of growth. In response, the Federal Reserve may raise interest rates to slow inflation. This rise in interest rates results in a slowdown of consumer spending and investing. The business cycle has four phases.

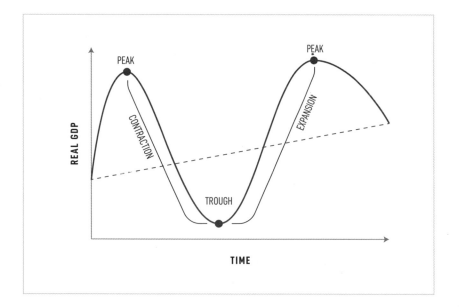

EXPANSION

During **expansion**, key economic indicators such as employment, wages, and supply and demand increase, inflation tops 2 percent, and GDP tops 3 percent. The stock market experiences a **bull market**—the condition where stock prices continue to rise—and business profits increase. A classic example of expansion took place during the "roaring twenties" when the economy grew at a rate of 42 percent.

PEAK

The month of a business cycle known as the **peak** is when the economy achieves maximum growth and prices are at a peak. The economy has hit its turning point where employment and new housing begin falling.

CONTRACTION

Economic growth falls below 2 percent and unemployment is 7 percent or higher during the **contraction** phase. The stock market begins experiencing a prolonged decrease in prices, known as a **bear market**.

TROUGH

When the economy reaches the end of its decline, it's in the **trough** phase.

Economic performance, GDP, and the purchasing value of money are all correlated. In the next chapter, we'll examine how money, inflation, and recession work in a market system.

DID YOU KNOW?

Canada, the United States, and Mexico generate 28 percent of the world's GDP, though they make up only 7 percent of the population.

The period from 1920 to 1929 in the United States is known as the **Roaring Twenties** because of extraordinary economic growth and sweeping social and political change. The 1920s saw the rise of the consumer economy in the United States, characterized by assembly lines and access to credit that made it possible for the country's middle class to purchase new products that made their lives easier. During this period, the country's wealth doubled. Department stores allowed customers to open lines of credit, and by the end of the decade, more than half of the country's automobiles were sold on credit.

Retro AdArchives/Alamy Stock

The decade was marked by advertising and chain stores that saw brands become national symbols of social class. This ushered in a change in marketing that saw advertisers creating demand instead of simply responding to it. The introduction of electric vacuum cleaners, washing machines, and irons changed the nature of housework, and the traditional household, by freeing up time in women's daily schedules. White-collar jobs as secretaries and stenographers opened up to them, and the 19th Amendment gave them the right to vote. The images of 1920s flappers spoke to the new freedoms some women gained during the era.

Middle-class African American families moved to Harlem, considered the Black cultural mecca of the time, and its artists, literature, and music signaled the start of the Harlem Renaissance. But the decade was also full of conflict, as the KKK grew in power and concepts of nativism and religious fundamentalism took hold. The era saw a clash of culture and ethics as the old battled with the new.

As the economic boom continued, signs of impending disaster loomed as stock prices remained highly inflated. When the Fed raised interest rates to try to curve speculation, it did so right as the economy had reached its peak. What resulted is what is still considered the worst financial disaster in world history.

CHAPTER 9:

MONEY, INFLATION, RECESSION, AND DEPRESSION

Money is the preferred medium of exchange among market economies; without it, transactions would still be taking place by bartering, which is time-consuming, cumbersome, and inefficient. The value of money in any society is determined by supply and demand. Inflation or deflation can result from changes in the value of money. When economic growth begins to decline, we generally say the economy is in a recession. We'll explore all of these concepts in this chapter.

– MONEY –

The **money supply** is controlled by the government and is the total amount of cash, coins, and balances in bank accounts in circulation in an economy. This supply of money is connected to all economic activity in society, and for that reason, economists track it, and the Federal Reserve's Board of Governors use the money supply to base monetary policy on.

In the United States, money is categorized in three different ways:

- The **monetary base** is the sum of all currency in circulation, including coins, currency, checking accounts, and deposits held by banks and other depository institutions with accounts held at the Federal Reserve.
- **M1** combines the monetary base and includes money held by the public in transaction deposits at depository institutions, such as commercial banks, savings and loan associations, and credit unions.
- **M2** includes M1, savings deposits, small-denomination time deposits (amounts less than $100,000), and retail money market mutual fund shares.

If the government increases the money supply by simply printing more, individual units of money lose value. The price and the value of money have an inverse relationship; when prices increase, the value of money decreases.

MILTON FRIEDMAN
(1912–2006)

Milton Friedman was born in New York City in 1912. He earned a BA from Rutgers University and an MA from the University of Chicago. In 1946, he earned his PhD from Columbia University.

Keystone/Stringer/Getty

In *A Theory of the Consumption Function*, Friedman argued against the Keynesian viewpoint that individuals and households adjust spending to reflect current income. Instead, Friedman said that annual consumption was a function of the average income they expected to receive over a few years. He called this the **permanent income**.

Friedman served as an adviser to President Richard Nixon and was president of the American Economic Association in 1967. He was awarded the Nobel Prize in economics in 1976.

Much of Friedman's work was based on price theory, a theory that explains how prices are determined. He is most recognized for monetarism, the school of thought that emphasizes the government's role in controlling the money supply. Friedman argued that if the Federal Reserve Board were required to increase the money supply at the same rate as real gross national product increased, inflation would disappear.

In *Capitalism and Freedom*, he made the case for relatively free markets, arguing for an end to licensing doctors, creating a negative income tax, and freely floating exchange rates, among other things. His 1980 book *Free to Choose*, cowritten with his wife, Rose Friedman, and the accompanying PBS TV series helped make him a household name.

"Inflation is taxation without representation."
–Milton Friedman

Inflation describes a state in the economy when prices are generally rising. It tells us how much more a set of goods and services cost than they used to. Economists list two different types of inflation: demand-pull and cost-push.

Demand-pull inflation occurs when the overall demand for goods and services in an economy increases more quickly than the economy's capacity to produce those goods and services. In demand-pull inflation, the unemployment rate is falling and the economy is close to full employment. When aggregate demand—the total demand for all domestically produced finished goods—is increasing at a rate that exceeds production capacity, firms will increase prices. A "hot" housing market is an example of demand-pull inflation.

Cost-push inflation occurs when aggregate supply—an economy's overall production of goods and services—decreases as a result of increases to production costs. This increase in the costs of any of the four factors of production inflates prices at a time when businesses are already operating at full capacity. In order to compensate for this, businesses pass the costs on to consumers in the form of price increases. The increase in prices for personal protective equipment (PPE) and antiviral cleaning products during a global pandemic is an example of cost-push inflation. The demand for these items during the pandemic became inelastic, meaning the quantity demanded remained constant even as the supply decreased. Another example of this was the oil crisis during the late 1970s, when demand for gas remained the same even as OPEC reduced its supply.

HOW INFLATION IS MEASURED
Consumer cost of living is dependent on the prices of goods and services and the percentage of a household budget spent to purchase them. In the United States, the Bureau of Labor Statistics (BLS) measures cost of living by conducting household surveys to identify a set of commonly purchased items, known as a basket of goods. They then monitor the cost of purchasing this set of items over

time. The **consumer price index** (CPI) measures the average change in prices paid by consumers over time for this basket of consumer goods and services. The basket of goods include items such as:

- Food and beverages—cereal, milk, coffee
- Housing—primary residences, furniture
- Clothing
- Transportation—new cars, airline fares, auto insurance
- Other goods and services—cigarettes, personal care services, funeral expenses

The CPI includes data on the spending habits of urban consumers. It does not include data on the spending habits of people in the military, prisons, or agricultural and rural households. The consumer price index also excludes prices set by the government as well as more volatile prices for food and energy that are affected by seasonal factors.

There are separate indexes for two groups or populations of consumers:

- The CPI for All Urban Consumers (CPI-U) is the index most often reported by the national media.
- The CPI for Urban Wage Earners and Clerical Workers (CPI-W) is the index most often used for wage escalation agreements.

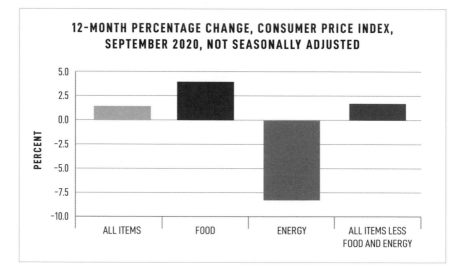

Source: U.S. Bureau of Labor Statistics

The BLS obtains these prices by visiting businesses and retail establishments to collect pricing on the approximately 80,000 items included in the basket.

The percentage change in CPI over a certain period of time is **consumer price inflation**, the most widely used measure of inflation.

HOW INFLATION AFFECTS INDIVIDUALS

In the simplest terms, inflation means you pay more for goods and services than you once did. Rising prices for certain assets, like homes, can be good if you're in the market to sell. The same holds true for stocks in your investment portfolio. But when income doesn't keep pace with inflation, or taxes on property outpaces a homeowner's ability to pay them, inflation can hurt individuals and the economy as a whole. Inflation can also hurt retirement plans if your savings and assets don't keep up with the cost of living. It also affects the amount of real income households have.

NOMINAL VS. REAL INCOME

Nominal income is income that has not been adjusted for inflation. Adjusting for inflation is important because it provides a more accurate measurement of what your income can buy, and therefore your purchasing power. **Real income** is calculated by subtracting the inflation rate per dollar from the real wage.

REAL INCOME FORMULA

Wages − (Wages x Inflation Rate) = Real Income

Some amount of inflation is typical, but very high and out-of-control inflation, a rate that exceeds 50 percent per month, known as **hyperinflation**, can quickly increase uncertainty.

VENEZUELA AND HYPERINFLATION

Hyperinflation usually happens during major economic collapses that include high unemployment and a significant drop in the production of goods and services.

By 2019, Venezuela's inflation was estimated in Reuters to be a staggering 9,585.5 percent. Yes, you read that right: over nine thousand percent.

What caused Venezuela's inflation to spiral out of control? In 2014, more than 90 percent of the Venezuelan economy was dependent on oil exports. Venezuelan president Hugo Chávez had been using the earnings from these exports to pay for the country's social programs. When the price of oil dropped, the demand for oil exports from Venezuela also dropped, and the cost of imports rose even as the value of its currency fell. In response, the new president, Nicolás Maduro, printed more money. By 2018, the exchange rate for one U.S. dollar to bolívares was 250,000.

Printing money made a bad situation worse, and the government continued to print more money as prices rose. The cycle this created led to Venezuela's hyperinflation.

– DEFLATION –

Deflation occurs when prices for goods and services are in decline. On the surface, this can be a good thing for consumers who end up paying lower prices for the things they need and want, but deflation leads to lower consumer spending overall, which in turn slows economic growth. Companies slow production, leading to wage cuts, layoffs, and increased unemployment. Deflation can also hurt borrowers and the financial markets that invest based on the expectation of rising prices.

Deflation can be caused by a number of factors. One factor is a decline in the total demand for goods and services coupled with increased productivity. Decreased government spending and the uncertainty that results in increased consumer savings can also lead to deflation.

— RECESSION —

Traditionally, a country is in a **recession** when it experiences two or more consecutive quarters of economic decline as measured by GDP and unemployment figures. The National Bureau of Economic Research (NBER), a private, nonprofit, nonpartisan organization that conducts economic research, uses monthly data to make its determination. The NBER includes income, manufacturing, and retail sales to determine whether an economy is in a recession.

DID YOU KNOW?

According to the World Bank, the global coronavirus pandemic and the shutdown measures to curtail its spread led the global economy into a severe contraction. The World Bank forecasted a 5.2 percent shrink in the global economy by the end of 2020, representing the deepest global recession since World War II.

TIME LINE:
RECESSIONS IN AMERICA

1797: The bubble burst on land speculation in the United States at the same time as market downturns in Great Britain, leading to the Panic of 1797. The events led to Congress passing the Bankruptcy Act of 1800, which restricted the ability of debtors to petition creditors. The law was repealed in 1803.

1857: Banks had invested in businesses that were failing, and the stock markets and railroads were also failing. The failure of the New York branch of the Ohio Life Insurance and Trust Company ushered in a fresh wave of panic that resulted in a recession that lasted for a year and a half.

1893: This recession, which lasted approximately four years, started with the failure of Reading Railroad and resulted in 12 percent unemployment.

1907: In response to this recession and the collapse of New York's Knickerbocker Trust Co., Congress created the Federal Reserve System.

1973–1975: This sixteen-month recession, which lasted from November 1973 to March 1975, was caused by OPEC, the Organization of Petroleum Exporting Countries. It quadrupled oil prices and led President Nixon to institute wage-price controls and remove the United States from the gold standard. The recession resulted in stagflation—five quarters of negative GDP growth.

2008–2009: This recession, known as the Great Recession, is seen as the worst and longest-lasting financial crisis in the United States since the 1929 Great Depression. The recession was triggered by the subprime mortgage crisis that led to a global bank crisis.

2020: As COVID-19-related illnesses swept across the country, cities and states went into lockdown, decimating small businesses across the nation. The restaurant, hotel, and airline industries were especially hard hit, as many Americans heeded state warnings to limit group and outdoor activities.

THE SUBPRIME MORTGAGE CRISIS
AND THE GREAT RECESSION

The 2008 collapse of Lehman Brothers, a global financial services firm, as a result of the subprime mortgage crisis is known as the greatest recession in North American history.

Subprime mortgages are typically extended to people with low credit scores and spotty credit histories. The word **subprime** refers to the below-average credit score of the borrowers. Because credit scores are one of the chief instruments used to identify lender risks, people with poor credit histories struggle to get approved for mortgages. Because they're seen as high risk, when they do get mortgages, they tend to only get them with much higher interest rates. Several types of subprime loans led to the industry's collapse.

Subprime mortgage loans were optional adjustable-rate mortgages (ARM) that allowed borrowers to choose what they would pay monthly, with the remainder being added to the loan's principal. After five years, the option disappeared, often exponentially increasing the cost of the loan. **Negative amortization loans** originated with low-interest payments, but the principal grew each month. **Balloon loans** allowed low monthly payments but required a balloon payment after five or seven years to pay off the loan's balance. And **ultra-long fixed-rate loans** extended conventional thirty-year mortgages to forty or fifty years.

People who previously weren't getting approved for loans were suddenly qualifying for them, and home ownership in the United States skyrocketed, for both high-risk and standard-risk home buyers. As demand for housing grew, housing prices also grew, along with the demand for subprime mortgage loans. Investment firms bought these loans and repackaged them as mortgage-backed securities. **Mortgage-backed securities** are bundles of home loans that investors buy from the banks that issued them.

By the mid-2000s, some economists had begun sounding the alarm about the growing housing bubble. And between 2004 and 2006, in an attempt to slow things down, the Federal Reserve raised the interest rate twelve times.

In 2007 as the recession began, the number of loans being issued declined. At the same time, interest rates were still rising, and many of the initial borrowers, unable to pay the higher interest rates, defaulted on their loans. Unemployment was also increasing as mortgage payments were ballooning. The housing market had begun to crash.

Banks were left with staggering loan losses as homeowners foreclosed on their homes. The recession resulted in a glut of foreclosed homes on the market that banks could not sell. As the number of investors pulling money out of banks and investment firms grew, those institutions began failing, too. The government soon created TARP—the Troubled Asset Relief Program—to bail out banks.

There is plenty of blame to go around for causing the subprime meltdown: credit agencies that approved nontraditional loans; mortgage brokers and investment firms that offered loans to high-risk individuals without the proper due diligence; and mortgage firms, such as Fannie Mae and Freddie Mac, that bought and guaranteed the incredibly risky loans.

The effects of the subprime mortgage crisis lingered for over a decade. Entire neighborhoods fell into disrepair as homeowners were evicted and homeowners association (HOA) fees went unpaid. The credit of many homeowners was ruined, as were the retirement plans of others.

DID YOU KNOW?

Between 2007 and 2010, approximately 3.8 million homes went into foreclosure in the United States.

SIGNS OF A RECESSION

The loss of manufacturing jobs is often the first sign that a recession is on the horizon. Because manufacturers receive orders months in advance, when those orders decline, the jobs associated with them do too. And when manufacturing hiring slows, that's an indication that the rest of the economy will as well. A drop in consumer demand begins to slow growth, and when sales decrease, the demand for labor does too, resulting in another reduction in hiring.

EFFECTS OF RECESSION ON SOCIETY

The number one way recessions impact society is through unemployment. The cyclical effect of unemployment is reduced demand, which results in a decrease in sales, which leads to more unemployment. Eventually, people are unable to pay their mortgages. And if a recession lasts for years, it can lead to a depression.

The traditional view of economics posits that the effects of a recession are short term and that following a recession, output returns to pre-recession rates. But current economic thinking is challenging that.

The economy took longer to recover after the Great Recession, taking almost a decade to begin showing signs of strong growth, prior to the pandemic. But researchers have found that recession can lead to **scarring**—long-lasting damage to individuals and the economy. Recessions can affect a family's access to pre-K education and early childhood nutrition, which have both been shown to have long-term effects on education and future wage-earning potential. After-school programs, access to health services, and housing disruptions also affect long-term earning potential. Individuals may also postpone college or opt out altogether, decreasing their potential lifelong earnings. And those individuals who enter the workforce during a recession will earn less than their non-recessionary counterparts.

– DEPRESSION –

An economic **depression** is a severe, long-term downturn in economic activity that lasts for three or more years or one that reduces GDP by at least 10 percent in a given year. Economic depressions are characterized by plummeting consumer confidence, reduced productivity, low or no inflation, high unemployment, and bankruptcies. The United States has had one depression in its history, the ten-year-long Great Depression. The economic impact of the Great Depression was far-reaching, and global markets suffered as a result.

The length and severity of a depression's economic downturn is what distinguishes it from a recession. Several negative events have to occur for a depression to take hold, and some economists believe that contractionary monetary policy—when a central bank uses interest rates on reserves to fight inflation, for example—during the late 1920s exacerbated the Great Depression.

As a result of laws and agencies that were put into place following the Great Depression, many economists believe that another depression of that scale is unlikely to happen again. Central banks are more likely to utilize expansionary monetary policy—lowering interest rates, for example—to stimulate the economy. The Federal Reserve also sets a specific inflation rate as its goal—inflation rate targeting—to help prevent the level of deflation associated with a depression. And finally, New Deal laws were implemented following the Great Depression. The creation of the Federal Deposit Insurance Corporation (FDIC) in 1933, for instance, guarantees bank deposits, which helps to maintain depositor confidence.

JOHN MAYNARD KEYNES (1883–1946)

John Maynard Keynes was born in Cambridge, England. His father was an economist and philosopher and his mother was the first female mayor. Keynes attended Eton and Cambridge University.

After the Versailles Peace Treaty, Keynes published *The Economic Consequences of the Peace*, where he criticized the war reparations Germany demanded and predicted Germans would later seek revenge. Keynes's *The General Theory of Employment, Interest and Money* is considered one of the most influential economics books in history. In it, he provided the basis for government jobs programs to address high unemployment.

Hulton Deutsch/Contributor/Getty

Keynes was initially a believer in the free market approach, but later began advocating that to stimulate demand in the face of recession, governments should increase spending and lower taxes. This would create jobs and increase buying power. This contradicted much of the belief at the time.

The Keynesian model of economics has fallen somewhat out of favor as economists become more concerned about inflation and unemployment.

CHAPTER 10:
ECONOMIC POLICY

E conomic policy refers to any government policy enacted to influence a country's economy. Monetary and fiscal policies are components of a country's economic policy. **Monetary policy** is directed by the Federal Reserve System while **fiscal policy** is directed by the president and Congress. Let's examine the components of each type of policy and how the Federal Reserve System operates within them.

> ## "Musicians burn through more cash than the Federal Reserve."
> *—Shawn Amos*

– THE FEDERAL RESERVE –

The Federal Reserve System (FRS), or "the Fed," is the central bank of the United States. It derives its power from Congress but is independent from political influence. Its goal is to ensure the country's financial stability. Congress establishes objectives for the Fed regarding employment and price stability, which is known as the **dual mandate**.

The Federal Reserve was created on December 23, 1913, when President Woodrow Wilson signed the Federal Reserve Act into law in response to the bank runs of 1907. The Fed conducts monetary policy and influences employment and inflation primarily through using its policy tools to affect the availability and cost of credit.

The Federal Reserve is comprised of three main entities:

- The Federal Open Market Committee (FOMC) is a twelve-member committee that establishes monetary policy and assess the risks to price stability and economic growth.
- Twelve Federal Reserve Banks, located in Atlanta, Boston, Chicago, Cleveland, Dallas, Kansas City, Minneapolis, New York, Philadelphia, Richmond, San Francisco, and St. Louis, provide accounts to banks, thrifts, and credit unions and make loans to these depository institutions. The banks also move currency and coin into and out of circulation and collect and process millions of checks each day.
- The Board of Governors or Federal Reserve Board (FRB), appointed by the president and confirmed by the Senate, is a seven-member agency that oversees the twelve reserve banks. The board members serve staggered, fourteen-year terms so that no one political party can control the board, and it is accountable to Congress.

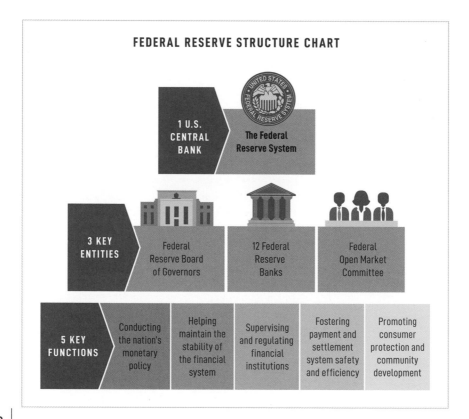

The Federal Reserve has five main functions:

- Conduct monetary policy to promote maximum employment, stabilize prices, and moderate long-term interest rates
- Promote the stability of the financial system
- Promote the soundness of financial institutions and monitor their effect on the financial system
- Foster payment and settlement system safety through services to the banking industry and the government
- Promote consumer protection

— MONETARY POLICY —

One of the central bank's key functions is to create monetary policy that influences the amount of money and credit in the United States and supports long-term economic growth. The goals of monetary policy include stabilizing prices and managing inflation, promoting employment, and moderating long-term interest rates.

The Federal Reserve's control over the **federal funds rate**—the target interest rate set by the FOMC—allows it to influence the short-term market interest rates. By adjusting short-term interest rates in response to changes in the economic outlook, the Federal Reserve also influences longer-term interest rates and prices. These interest rate adjustments then affect household and business spending decisions.

For example, when interest rates decrease, borrowing becomes cheaper, so households are more willing to buy goods and services. Businesses are also in a better position to hire more workers and purchase items that will help them expand their businesses. This behavior increases demand for goods and services, which, in turn, pushes wages and other costs higher, influencing inflation.

The Federal Reserve has an inflation target of 2 percent, a goal consistent with the consumer price index—the price based on the basket of goods described earlier—and with maximum employment and price stability in mind. When inflation is high, the cost of everyday essentials like food, gas, and rent increase, creating additional burdens on individuals and households. On the other hand, very low inflation can signal a weakening economy as consumer demand for goods and services slows.

The central bank uses two types of monetary policy to achieve its goals: expansionary and contractionary.

"Money often costs too much."
—Ralph Waldo Emerson

EXPANSIONARY MONETARY POLICY

The goal of **expansionary monetary policy** is to help reduce unemployment and keep the economy out of a recession. The central bank achieves this by giving banks more money to lend. When banks have more money to lend, they lower interest rates, making the cost of borrowing cheaper. When it's cheaper to borrow, individuals will increase purchases, firms will buy more equipment, and economic growth will be spurred.

EVERYDAY EXAMPLE

During the Great Recession, the Federal Reserve employed expansionary policy, cutting the discount rate—the interest rate the federal government charges to banks—until it was zero. When the economy remained weak, it began a four-year run of purchasing government securities to the tune of $3.7 trillion.

The Fed can also reduce reserve requirements—the minimum amount commercial banks are required to reserve with the central bank. This reduction in reserves releases additional funds banks can lend their clients.

Finally, the Fed may opt to purchase large amounts of government bonds and other securities from institutional investors in order to add cash to the economy.

JANET YELLEN
(1946–)

Janet Yellen is an American economist and the first woman to hold the position of chair of the Board of Governors of the Federal Reserve System. Yellen graduated from Brown University and received her PhD in economics from Yale. She was an assistant professor of economics at Harvard University and worked as an economist for the Federal Reserve Board of Governors from 1978 to 1980 before going on to teach macroeconomics and conduct research at the Haas School of Business at the University of California, Berkeley.

Alexandros Michailidis/Shutterstock

Yellen served as a member of the Board of Governors of the Federal Reserve System from 1994 to 1997, when she left to head President Bill Clinton's Council of Economic Advisors. She was appointed vice chair of the Board of Governors in 2010.

In 2014, President Barack Obama nominated Yellen to head the Federal Reserve System. Though Republicans worried that Yellen would focus on reducing unemployment and not controlling inflation, she was confirmed by a Senate vote in January 2014 by the smallest confirmation margin for a head of the Fed in history. She was the first Democrat in nearly thirty years to become chair.

Yellen's tenure was noted for its job and wage growth, even as interest rates remained low. A Keynesian economist, Yellen believed that government regulations were necessary to allow economic markets to function correctly. During her tenure, she tightened financial and banking regulations.

She was succeeded by Jerome H. Powell when President Donald Trump did not nominate her for a second term. She was the first chair in almost forty years not to receive a second term.

On November 30, 2020, President Biden nominated Yellen for secretary of the Treasury. She was confirmed on January 25, 2021, and sworn in the following day by Vice President Kamala Harris.

CONTRACTIONARY MONETARY POLICY

When inflation is too high, banks use **contractionary monetary policy** to reduce the money supply and restrict lending to banks. If you're thinking that if the Fed decreases short-term interest rates to help expand the economy, then they'll probably increase the rates to contract it, you're right. When the Fed increases the interest rate to commercial banks, those banks in turn raise the interest rates they charge their clients. The Fed will also raise reserve requirements, decreasing the money supply in the economy. And finally, the Federal Reserve can reduce the amount of money circulated in the economy by selling government securities to investors.

– FISCAL POLICY –

Fiscal policy refers to a government's tax and spending policies established by Congress and the administration. The goal of fiscal policy is to achieve healthy annual economic growth of 2 to 3 percent. Prior to the Great Depression, the government had a laissez-faire, hands-off approach to managing the economy, but the Great Depression underscored the need for government policies that would help manage the economy and assist citizens in times of need.

As with monetary policy, there are two types of fiscal policy: contractionary and expansionary.

"Taxes are what we pay for civilized society."

–Oliver Wendell Holmes Jr.

CONTRACTIONARY FISCAL POLICY

Contractionary fiscal policy increases taxes and decreases government spending in an effort to slow economic growth. Why would a government want to slow economic growth? When growth gets beyond 2 to 3 percent, it creates inflation, lowers unemployment below the natural rate, and makes it hard for businesses to find employees.

Contractionary policies aren't used as often as expansionary ones. For one, few individuals enjoy tax hikes. In fact, promising to lower taxes has become the hallmark of political campaigning because those who make those promises tend to get elected. And because tax hikes are so unpopular, governments frequently face budget deficits.

EXPANSIONARY FISCAL POLICY

During times of recession, Congress uses **expansionary fiscal policy** to provide relief to businesses and individuals in an effort to end economic contraction. Expansionary fiscal policies need to boost the economy while keeping inflation as low as possible. When a government uses expansionary policies, it spends more money than it collects through taxes. Expansionary fiscal policy includes things like tax cuts, unemployment benefits, and social services like SNAP benefits. Economic stimulus checks sent to taxpayers are a type of expansionary fiscal policy. Those funds go directly to consumers, who, in theory, return it to the economy by buying more goods and services.

Unlike state and local governments, which are mandated to operate with a balanced budget, the federal government can tax and spend when needed. This increases deficit spending, a situation where purchases exceed income. When the government doesn't have the cash to fund its own spending, it funds its debts by issuing **fixed-income securities**. A security is a financial instrument with monetary value, and a fixed-income security is one where the return on investment is the same, or fixed, over time.

Fixed-income government-issued securities include Treasury bonds, Treasury notes, and Treasury bills. These securities are issued by the federal government and the debt is paid back at regular intervals called **coupon payments**. These securities are considered low-risk investments.

TREASURY BONDS

Treasury bonds, or T-bonds, pay the highest interest rates, have a twenty- or thirty-year maturity, and pay out fixed-interest payments every six months. They are issued monthly, directly by the U.S. Treasury, and sold in multiples of $100.

TREASURY NOTES

Treasury notes mature between two to ten years and are paid out every six months until maturity. Treasury notes are sold in multiples of $100.

TREASURY BILLS

Treasury Bills have the shortest term of the government fixed-income securities with a maturity date of one year or less. The minimum purchase for treasury bills is $100.

FISCAL POLICY IN ACTION: THE CARES ACT

On March 27, 2020, in response to the COVID-19 pandemic, President Donald Trump signed an economic stimulus package into law. Known as the CARES Act (Coronavirus Aid, Relief, and Economic Security), the law provided much-needed financial support and emergency relief to individuals, small businesses, large corporations, hospitals and public health operations, and state and local governments.

The CARES Act provided an estimated $300 billion in cash payments to individuals and households making less than $99,000 and $198,000 annually, respectively. The act also included an estimated $260 billion in extra unemployment assistance to individuals who were unemployed or underemployed as a direct result of COVID-19. The act allowed for self-employed and gig workers to apply for unemployment, which they previously had been unable to do. For businesses, the CARES Act created a forgivable loan program for companies with fewer than five hundred employees and made it easier for them to keep employees on the payroll.

The economic stimulus package, the largest in U.S. history to that point, was not without its problems. Months-long delays in receiving unemployment benefits, funding running out for small business assistance, and the fact that months after the first stimulus check millions of Americans remained unemployed meant the stimulus package, for some, was too little and too late.

The CARES Act came with a hefty $2 trillion price tag, but the question for many economists wasn't whether the United States could afford to pass the package, but whether it could afford not to.

— GOVERNMENT SPENDING —

Why does the government spend and where do they get the money they spend? Where do our taxes go?

In the fiscal year 2019, the federal government spent $4.4 trillion, about 21 percent of the gross domestic product (GDP). This spending was financed by revenues and borrowing. Sources of revenue for the federal government include:

- Individual income taxes (50 percent)
- Corporate income taxes (7 percent)
- Payroll taxes (36 percent)
- Federal excise taxes, or taxes on goods and services (2.9 percent)
- Other revenues—customs duties, estate taxes, and earnings from the Federal Reserve System

Of that $4.4 trillion in spending, $984 billion was financed through borrowing.

THE BULK OF GOVERNMENT SPENDING

The bulk of government spending is in three areas: Social Security; Medicare, Medicaid, Children's Health Insurance Program (CHIP), and ACA (the Affordable Care Act) marketplace subsidies; and defense spending.

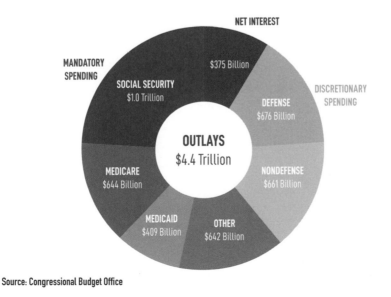

Source: Congressional Budget Office

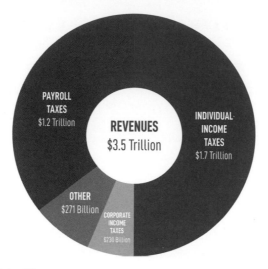

PAYROLL TAXES
$1.2 Trillion

REVENUES
$3.5 Trillion

INDIVIDUAL INCOME TAXES
$1.7 Trillion

OTHER
$271 Billion

CORPORATE INCOME TAXES
$230 Billion

Source: Congressional Budget Office

SOCIAL SECURITY

Social Security is a federal program that provides income benefits to eligible retirees and individuals who are unable to work because of a disability. In 2019, the government spent approximately $1 trillion in Social Security.

MEDICARE, MEDICAID, CHIP, AND ACA MARKETPLACE SUBSIDIES

In 2019, Medicare, Medicaid, the Children's Health Insurance Program (CHIP), and the Affordable Care Act (ACA) marketplace subsidies accounted for $1.1 trillion in spending, or 25 percent of the federal budget. Approximately $651 billion was spent on Medicare, health coverage for seniors and those with disabilities. The remainder of spending went to Medicaid (health insurance for low-income individuals) and CHIP (health insurance for children). The final expenditure in this category provides subsidies that lower premiums for individuals who get their health insurance through the ACA marketplace.

DEFENSE SPENDING

The government spends $697 billion, or 16 percent of its budget, on defense and security-related activities. Expenses in this category include the costs of operating the Defense Department and supporting military operations.

INTEREST AND SOCIAL SAFETY NET PROGRAMS

The federal government spends less than a fifth of its budget on interest on debt and social safety net programs. Interest on debt accounts for $375 billion in spending, or 8 percent of the budget. Social safety net programs, such as SNAP (food stamps), school meals, low-income housing assistance, unemployment insurance, and child-protection programs, also account for about 8 percent of government spending.

In 2018, government safety net programs kept an estimated 37 million people out of poverty. Without Social Security and safety net spending, the poverty rate would nearly double from 12.8 percent to about 24.0 percent.

The remaining federal spending supports public services: providing health care for veterans; paying retirement benefits to retired federal employees; ensuring safe food and drugs; protecting the environment; investing in education; conducting scientific and medical research; and maintaining basic infrastructure, such as roads, bridges, and airports. Less than 1 percent of the federal budget goes to support international programs such as humanitarian aid.

BUDGET DEFICITS

Inflation is one of the key problems with budget deficits. During a budget deficit, the Federal Reserve may release more money into the economy, which accelerates inflation. Increasing inflation may lead to recession, as the price of borrowing increases and purchasing slows.

Sustained budget deficits can result in persistent use of inflationary monetary policy. Fiscal policies can help reduce budget deficits by increasing taxes and reducing government spending to promote economic growth.

THE TAX MAN COMETH

In the United States, **taxes** are imposed on individuals and corporations on net income at the federal, state, and local levels. Sales taxes are charged on purchases and vary from state to state and within counties in a state.

> ## "Nothing is certain but death and taxes."
>
> *–Benjamin Franklin*

Individuals who work for an employer get paid by that employer either by direct deposit or a physical paycheck that is cashed or deposited in a bank or credit union. Your pay stub, whether electronic or physical, shows everything the government deducts from your paycheck in the form of taxes, investments (like 401k), and other employee benefits such as health insurance. Taxes taken from your check provide revenue to the federal government. These taxes include:

- Federal income taxes
- State taxes
- FICA—The Federal Insurance Contributions Act (FICA) requires everyone who works to contribute to Social Security and Medicare. Every employee contributes 6.2 percent of gross income to Social Security and employers match that. Self-employed individuals pay a total of 12.4 percent into Social Security. The government also requires workers to contribute 1.45 percent of their gross income to Medicare. Employers match this as well, and self-employed individuals are responsible for paying the full 2.9 percent.

If you've opted to participate in your employer's 401k plan, you'll also see that deduction taken from your check. But that deduction isn't made by the government. A 401k plan is an employer-sponsored retirement plan that allows a payroll deduction of a portion of your salary to be divested into long-term investments. One of the key benefits of a 401k plan is employer-matching contributions that increase the value of the plan and reduce your taxable income. In addition, 401k plans typically offer investment opportunities in mutual funds and stocks. Speaking of stocks . . .

STRANGE PROJECTS
FUNDED BY TAX DOLLARS

Taxes are the price we pay to live in a society that provides benefits to its citizens. Taxes help pay to maintain the roads we use to commute to and from work, the public libraries and parks we visit, and the schools that educate our children. But some of the projects taxes have funded over the years are a little harder to explain. Here are just a few examples.

- A 2016 program funded by a grant from the National Science Foundation and the Department of Defense's Office of Naval Research paid to program computers to binge-watch hundreds of hours of television to help them predict and understand human behavior. The results of the $460,000 study were inconclusive.
- In the 1960s, the CIA spent $10 million implanting microphones and radio transmitters in cats, hoping to use them as surveillance cats who would pass by security at the Soviet Embassy undetected. The project failed, most likely because no one can tell cats what to do.
- The National Endowment for the Humanities (NEH) provided $450,000 in funding to create a documentary about Tupperware. The documentary explored things like positive thinking and "housewifely entrepreneurship."
- Beginning in 2010, the National Institutes of Health (NIH) received over $350,000 to study the sexual habits of quails (yes, the bird) that were hooked on cocaine. Believe it or not, quail mating is somewhat similar to human mating, and studying the coked-up interactions were used to help scientists better understand addiction in humans.
- In 1943, the national Research Defense Committee gave inventor and psychologist B. F. Skinner $25,000 to train pigeons how to guide missiles. Although Skinner was apparently successful in training the pigeons, the military ultimately abandoned the project, code named "Project Pigeon."
- Honorable Mention: In 2006, Congress earmarked—funneled money to a politician's pet project—$500,000 for the Sparta Teapot Museum of Craft and Design. At the time, Sparta, North Carolina, had a population of 18,000. The museum's creators had hoped it would become a "teapot hall of fame." Federal tax dollars did not end up going to the project, which was supported by state tax dollars and private funding until it closed in 2010.

— STOCKS —

A **stock**, also known as a **share** or **equity**, is a financial instrument that means ownership in a company or corporation. Once you purchase a stock, you become a **shareholder**, signifying a claim on a corporation's assets. As a shareholder in that corporation, you own a slice of it.

The two main types of stocks are common and preferred. **Common stock**, also known as equities, gives shareholders voting rights, while **preferred stock** does not. Owners of preferred stock don't get a say on who's elected to the board and they have no input into corporate policy. But they are often paid **dividends**, a portion of a company's earnings, each quarter. Most people buy shares of common stock, and common stocks tend to perform better than preferred stock.

THE HISTORY OF STOCK EXCHANGES

Exchanges date back to the Middle Ages, but the first modern stock trading began with the Dutch East India Company, which sent people to Asia to bring goods back to Europe. Because not all of the expeditions returned, the company sold shares to investors as a way to group liability in the event that ships were lost at sea or were victims of pirating.

The Dutch East India Company issued its first paper shares in 1602. This was the first time shareholders were allowed to buy, sell, and trade stock with other investors. The idea of diversifying risk became so popular that selling shares spread to France, Portugal, and Spain and eventually ended up in England.

In 1773, a group of traders met at a London coffee house to plan their stock trading. Eventually, they took over the coffee house and began calling it a stock exchange, launching the first-ever stock exchange: the London Stock Exchange. The idea made its way across the pond, and years later, the American colonies began their first exchange in Philadelphia, Pennsylvania.

In May 1792, the market opened on Wall Street with twenty-four supply brokers, who signed the Buttonwood agreement. On March 8, 1817, the group renamed itself the New York Stock Exchange and Exchange Board, launching what would someday become one of the most influential exchanges in the world.

A company issues shares to raise money to help fund growth. When a company is in the early stages of development, they typically have few assets to use as collateral to finance expansion. These start-ups raise capital by either borrowing money or selling shares, a process known as **equity financing**. When the start-up is ready to make their offer in public, they do it through what's called an **initial public offering**, or IPO. The IPO changes the company from being privately held to one whose shares will be held by the shareholders who publicly purchase the stocks when it's on the market. The number of outstanding shares refers to the number of shares of a company's stock held by its shareholders.

A company lists its shares on the **stock exchange**, the marketplace (physical and/or virtual) where shares are offered for sale to the public. The **stock market** refers to the buyers and sellers who buy and sell stocks.

"Rule #1: Don't lose money. Rule #2: Don't forget Rule #1."

—Warren Buffett

THE STOCK MARKET

The stock market allows hundreds of thousands of market participants to buy, sell, and exchange stock and other financial instruments. It is regulated by the Securities and Exchange Commission (SEC), which also oversees the stock exchanges and the companies that sell securities. In addition to companies that offer shares and investors who buy them, other participants in the stock markets include:

- *Stockbrokers*, who are licensed professionals who act as intermediaries, buying and selling financial instruments on behalf of investors.
- *Investment bankers*, who help raise capital for corporations by issuing stock and managing initial public offerings. JP Morgan Chase, Deutsche Bank, and Goldman Sachs are examples of firms that employ investment bankers.
- *Portfolio managers*, who act on behalf of clients to invest a collection of financial investments, including stocks, for their clients.

EIGHT OF THE LARGEST IPOS IN HISTORY

An IPO (initial public offering) allows a company to raise capital by offering the public a percentage of the company's ownership. The companies on this list are notable for raising billions of dollars the day they went public.

- German telecommunications company Deutsche Telekom AG went public on November 17, 1996. The company, which owns T-Mobile and T-Systems, raised a little over $13 billion in its IPO.
- On March 19, 2008, debit and credit card processing company Visa Inc. made an IPO of 406 million shares of common stock priced at $44 per share, at the time becoming the largest IPO in U.S. history. Visa raised $17.3 billion on its first day of trading.
- Facebook's IPO was a feature story for weeks in the run-up to the event. And when the social media giant went public on May 1, 2012, it raised over $16 billion.
- Tokyo-based NTT DoCoMo Inc., whose name is an abbreviation of "do communications over the mobile network," is Japan's leading mobile phone operator. On October 22, 1998, the communications giant went public, raising almost $18.4 billion.
- Enel S.p.A. is an Italian gas and electricity manufacturer that does business in thirty-four countries. The company raised almost $17.4 billion in their IPO on November 1, 1999.
- Listed on both the Shanghai and the Hong Kong Stock Exchanges, the Multinational Chinese banking company ICBC (Industrial and Commercial Bank of China) went public on October 20, 2006, and raised almost $19.1 billion. Three months later, ICBC exercised what's known as a "greenshoe option," which allowed them to issue additional shares that lifted their IPO to $21.9 billion.
- On November 16, 2010, a year after emerging from bankruptcy, American auto manufacturer GM (General Motors) raised $20.1 billion dollars in its IPO, the largest IPO for a U.S.-based company.
- Online e-commerce giant Alibaba Group Holding holds the current record for the largest IPO. When it went public on September 18, 2014, the company raised $21.8 billion. Alibaba exercised an option to sell more shares a few days later, bringing the total raised to $25 billion.

The stock market allows publicly traded companies to raise the funds they need to grow and innovate. The stock market also allows individual investors to own shares in successful companies.

Because stocks are a liquid asset—assets that can be converted to cash in a short amount of time—they're an attractive option for investors. Assets such as property, for example, are not liquid and are more difficult to convert to cash.

Changes in the stock market can have a significant effect on the economy. Strong stock market performance can help ensure business owners and individuals will participate, while a drop in share prices can spell economic doom.

Because the stock market shows us how well a selection of companies are performing and provides insight into investors' outlook, the market can be an indicator of how well the economy is doing. It can also create growth, as the capital earned from offering stock allows businesses to invest in technology, resources, and innovation that they wouldn't otherwise be able to.

Though movement in the market can affect the economy, the stock market is not the economy. This is evident during periods where the stock market is booming, yet unemployment remains high.

Several factors can affect the stock market's performance, including the political climate, interest rates, investor confidence, and worldwide events. If the outlook for the country's future with regard to jobs, production, and business profit is positive, the stock market will generally perform well. When the outlook is negative, the stock market will often fall. When the evening news anchorperson talks about the Dow Jones falling, they're talking about the drop in prices of the shares of the companies that make up the index.

In general, if the outlook is negative and people and firms believe that the economy will be heading south, they tend to sell stock because Treasurer bonds are more reliable. Conversely, when there's confidence in the economy, politicians, and the future, people tend to buy stock, expecting more reward for the risk they're taking.

The market can help investors combat inflation by earning them an average of 7 percent annually. These earnings outpace the rate of inflation and reward investors for forgoing low-yielding savings accounts and bonds.

On the other hand, significant losses in the stock market not only affect individuals' 401k plans, but they also reduce consumer spending and can cause a slowdown in economic growth.

Of course, these effects are more intensely felt by individuals who own stocks. In fact, according to an April 2020 Gallup poll, only a small majority of Americans, 55 percent, own stock. The richest 10 percent of households controlled 84 percent of the total value of stocks in 2016.

THE WORST ECONOMIC EVENT IN THE HISTORY OF THE WORLD

On Thursday, October 24, 1929, investors began trading a record 12.9 million shares on the stock market. By Monday, October 28, now known as Black Monday, the Dow Jones Industrial Average had plunged almost 13 percent. On Black Tuesday, the market fell another 12 percent. Following that panic, people rushed to banks, withdrawing funds in bank runs, and investors were unable to withdraw money because banks had invested in the market.

Economists attribute the stock market crash to several things. For one, the market and the public had been overconfident. The "roaring twenties" had seen a rise in income, investment, and credit extended to American families. Many bought stock "on margin" to allow them to borrow from stockbrokers with as little as 10 percent of the share's value. Some had been warning for years that stocks were overpriced and that a collapse was inevitable. Still, no one could have predicted the depths to which the country would fall in what became known as the Great Depression.

MARKET INDEXES

Analysts use market indexes to follow the performance of markets and measure the performance of a group of stocks. Major indexes include the Dow Jones Industrial Average, the NASDAQ, and the S&P 500. When the average value of all stocks in an index is down from the previous day, the index has dropped. When the value has increased, the index has risen.

DOW JONES INDUSTRIAL AVERAGE

The Dow Jones Industrial Average, or "the Dow," measures the performance of thirty large companies, including American Express, Coca-Cola, Nike, and Procter & Gamble.

NASDAQ

NASDAQ can refer to both a stock exchange and an index. The index includes a hundred of the largest domestic and international companies listed on the NASDAQ exchange, including Warner Music Group, Facebook, Costco, and the Scholastic Corporation.

S&P 500

The S&P 500 measures the performance of five hundred large U.S. companies, including Apple, Johnson & Johnson, Amazon, and 3M.

STOCK EXCHANGES

The New York Stock Exchange (NYSE) and NASDAQ (National Association of Securities Dealers Automated Quotations) are the world's largest stock exchanges. Hong Kong, India, Australia, London, and other major cities throughout the European Union also have stock exchanges. Exchanges operate like auctions, with traders bidding share prices up or down depending on how well a company performs.

Stock exchanges charge a fee for their services and earn revenue from the transaction fees from the trades made on their platforms. They also earn revenue from listing fees they charge companies making IPOs. Buyers and sellers place bids to buy and sell in an auction process.

Stock market corrections occur when market prices decline less than 10 percent. If that decline occurs during one day, the market is said to have crashed. A **bear market** occurs when prices fall more than 20 percent. When stock prices are rising and are expected to continue to rise, it is known as a **bull market**.

SUPPLY AND DEMAND IN THE STOCK MARKET

Just as the law of supply and demand determines prices in our microeconomic examples, the same holds true for the stock market. The demand for stocks is affected by the state of the economy. When the economy is doing well or when the future outlook for the economy is positive, the demand for stocks increases. Stock prices and the demand for stocks fluctuate based on the market and economic conditions, but the supply of stocks is more consistent.

A **stock quote** is the price of a stock on the stock exchange. The stock quote is a quick way for a potential investor to check a stock's price and other relevant information, including the following:

- **Company name:** The company whose stocks are being traded
- **Stock exchange:** The exchange where the stock is traded
- **Ticker symbol:** A string of letters that identifies the stock
- **Current price:** The most recent price
- **Price change:** The percent change in price during the trading day
- **Market cap:** The value of all of a company's publicly traded shares
- **Price-earnings ratio:** The price of a single share divided by the earnings per share for the previous twelve months
- **Dividend yield:** A calculation of the next twelve months of income dividend by current share price

CHAPTER II

THE ECONOMY'S IMPACT ON SOCIETY

W e've examined several microeconomic and macroeconomic concepts up to this point, and in this chapter, we're going to look at the social implications of some of these concepts. I'll do that by first talking about unemployment, explaining the various types, sharing some statistics, and examining how unemployment affects individuals, firms, and society as a whole. Then I'll talk about social issues in the areas of gender, racial discrimination, and global warming and the effect these issues have on individuals and economies.

– UNEMPLOYMENT –

We've learned that several factors contribute to unemployment. High interest rates, recessions, and natural or man-made disasters can all lead to staggering rates of unemployment. **Unemployment** officially occurs when someone who is willing and legally able to work actively seeks work but is unable to find it.

Unemployment has implications at both micro- and macroeconomic levels. For individuals and households, unemployment leads to financial difficulties that may manifest in extremes such as hunger and homelessness. For society as a whole, periods of high, sustained unemployment lead to decreased demand for goods and services, which in turn reduces business profits and the ability to hire and keep workers. But some level of unemployment is natural and expected, so economists break unemployment down into three categories: cyclical, frictional, and structural.

The Bureau of Labor Statistics gathers data on unemployment in the United States based on estimates of confirmed employment, hours, and earnings of workers on payrolls.

INCOME INEQUALITY

Income inequality refers to the uneven distribution of income among a population. Prior to the global pandemic that weakened every economy around the world, the United States had been experiencing the longest U.S. economic expansion in history. Between 2008 and 2018, the number of billionaires in the United States doubled from 267 to 607.

During that same period, the number of people on the government's Supplemental Nutrition Assistance Program (SNAP) was up by 40 percent. Also in the United States:

- The top 10 percent of income earners average more than nine times as much as the bottom 90 percent. Those in the top 0.1 percent are making 196 times the income of the bottom 90 percent.
- Although women make up half of the country's workforce, they represent just 27 percent of the top 10 percent of income earners.
- Income inequality in the United States is the highest among all G7 nations.
- The income gap between Black and white Americans is worse today than it was twenty years ago.
- In the last quarter of 2018, the median white worker earned 28 percent more than the median Black worker and thirty-five times more than the median Latino worker.

The growing income gap in the United States paints a grim picture about the future of income trends in this country. One factor attributed to the widening income gap is the decline of labor unions. Since the 1940s and 1950s, when unions were at their peak, membership has declined to less than 11 percent. Racial discrimination in education, hiring, and pay also contribute to the widening income gap.

Income inequality has a negative long-term effect on GDP. A study by the Economic Policy Institute shows that income inequality suppresses growth, shifting increasingly larger shares of household and business spending to households that save. Some economists believe that expansionary macroeconomic policies that include lowering interest rates and increasing government spending have the potential to spur wage growth for low- and middle-wage workers, raising living standards in the process.

CYCLICAL UNEMPLOYMENT

Cyclical unemployment occurs as a result of fluctuations in the economy, such as a recession. When demand for goods and services decreases, firms react by decreasing production.

To see an example of this, let's revisit Tamika and T&K Bakery. A recession has resulted in a 50 percent decrease in the number of cupcakes and cookies T&K bakery sells. Up until now, Tamika has managed to hold on to her two workers, Amina and Michael, but with her sales dropping every day, she realizes she'll need to let one of them go. Michael has been with Tamika since she opened T&K Bakery, so Tamika makes the difficult decision to let Amina go. Amina, a single mother of a young son, has some savings and will be able to collect unemployment while she looks for work, but things will be difficult.

Amina is a casualty of cyclical unemployment. She is going to have to tighten her belt now that she's lost her job, and to save money, she says goodbye to her daily morning latte from her local coffee shop and her twice weekly dinners out with her son. The cycle continues as the recession causes others to cut the number of lattes they consume daily, and soon the coffee shop begins laying off employees too.

FRICTIONAL UNEMPLOYMENT

Frictional unemployment occurs when workers who have voluntarily left their jobs haven't yet found new ones. These workers are in the process of moving from one job to another. Frictional unemployment is caused by temporary changes in a person's life or situation and includes recent graduates. There is always some level of frictional unemployment in a society.

STRUCTURAL UNEMPLOYMENT

Structural unemployment occurs as a result of changes in an industry where technology causes a mismatch between available jobs and workers with the skills to perform them. An example of structural unemployment can be seen in factories in the United States and around the world, where machine technology is replacing human workers at increasing rates. The agricultural industry is a good example of structure unemployment because agricultural mechanization, using machinery to mechanize farm work, replaces human laborers.

When skill gaps exist—that is, when laid-off workers are unable to get the training and skills they need to take on the more technical positions—long-term structural unemployment occurs. As unskilled workers stay out of the workforce, they may remain unemployed, leading to a higher rate of natural unemployment.

NATURAL UNEMPLOYMENT

Natural unemployment is the minimum unemployment rate that exists in a healthy economy. Frictional and structural unemployment are both a part of natural unemployment: natural unemployment includes individuals who lack the skills need to get work and those in between jobs. The natural unemployment rate in the United States is between 4 and 6 percent.

OUTSOURCING, UNEMPLOYMENT, AND THE ECONOMY

Outsourcing happens when firms hire workers outside of the country's home base. Outsourcing allows companies to compete, keeping labor costs low by paying workers in emerging markets less than they would pay workers from the companies' home countries. Here are some statistics about outsourcing:

- The United States outsources approximately 300,000 jobs annually.
- Sixty percent of outsourced work is related to IT (information technology).
- In 2017, 84.2 percent of outsourced jobs originated from the United States.
- In 2019, 14.3 million jobs were outsourced.

Despite reduced costs for companies, outsourcing leads to unemployment in the country of origin, and over the past several years, American workers and politicians have decried the increase in outsourcing in the United States.

UNEMPLOYMENT AND THE STOCK MARKET

During the latter part of 2020, the stock market surged, even as unemployment hit record highs, COVID-19 deaths surpassed the 200,000 mark, and anti-racism protests spread across the United States. The United States had officially entered a recession, its first since the Great Recession a decade prior, but the S&P 500 gained an unprecedented 43 percent after a fifty-day rally. The disconnect between the stock market and unemployment had many scratching their heads and wondering how such dismal employment news led to gains in the stock market.

To understand why, we have to understand what stocks represent. Stocks represent ownership in companies. Investors look toward what they think will happen to the value of that stock in the future, and despite the nation's turmoil during that time, investors seemed to be hopeful about the future.

Investors were optimistic about states reopening and a potential vaccine on the horizon, both of which would lead to a return in consumer spending. They didn't see a risk of long-term damage. Only time will tell what the long-term effects of the deadly pandemic toll will be on society, the markets, and the world.

> ## "When it comes to the environment, the invisible hand never picks up the check."
>
> *–Kim Stanley Robinson*

– THE GENDER PAY GAP –

The increasing participation of women in the U.S. labor force in the second half of the twentieth century was a major factor in the country's economic growth. In 1950, there were 18.4 million women in the workforce, and they accounted for about a third of the labor force. By 2015, that number had increased to 73.5 million

GENDER AND ECONOMIC EMPOWERMENT: A GLOBAL VIEW

Despite the economic and social gains women have made around the world over the past few decades, many barriers still exist to women gaining full participation in the workforce, wage equality, and economic empowerment. According to UN Women, a United Nations-based organization that champions gender equality worldwide:

- Over 2.7 billion women are legally prevented from working in jobs that have been traditionally held by men.
- In 2018, 104 of 189 economies assessed for gender inequality in the workforce had laws on the books that prevented women from working specific jobs; in 18 economies, husbands can legally prevent their wives from working outside the home.
- The labor force participation rate for women ages 25 to 54 was 63 percent, compared to 94 percent for men.
- When they are allowed to work, women earn 77 percent of what men earn.
- Only 12.8 percent of agricultural landowners are women.
- The economic cost of violence and sexual harassment in the workforce is estimated at $12 trillion USD annually.

In addition, women are more likely to be unemployed than men, are paid less, and disproportionately bear the brunt of unpaid domestic and childcare work. But healthy, growing economies and sustainable development require women's contributions. When women are empowered through education, access to resources, and equal-paying work, entire nations benefit.

and women made up 46.8 percent of the overall workforce. According to the Bureau of Labor Statistics, that percentage will increase to 47.2 by the year 2024.

Over the next decade, the labor force will become even more racially and ethnically diverse, with Hispanic women projected to account for 18.1 percent of the women's labor force by 2024. As women continue to enter the workforce, gender wage gap disparities persist. Fundamental shifts in policy that have resulted in an increasing wealth gap overall has had an even greater impact on women.

A 2018 Pew Research Center analysis of full- and part-time workers in the United States revealed that women earned 85 percent of what men earned. There are many reasons the gender pay gap persists. Some of the gap is explained by differences in work experience, education, and occupational segregation— segregation of work based on gender stereotypes. But other reasons persist, and these include gender discrimination, family caregiving responsibilities, and the overrepresentation of women in lower-paying occupations.

An IMF study found that inclusive fiscal policies, such as subsidizing childcare and offering paid parental leave, could create more economic opportunities for women. These gender-responsive policies can help increase productivity, which in turn would help develop sustainable economic growth.

— THE SOCIAL AND ECONOMIC IMPACT — OF MODERN-DAY SLAVERY

Globally, forced labor generates $150 billion in annual profits, more than double the profits of Fannie Mae, the world's most profitable company. And without knowing it, many consumers contribute to this economic crime.

The U.S. State Department defines modern-day slavery, or forced labor, as the "range of activities—recruiting, harboring, transporting, providing, or obtaining—involved when a person uses force or physical threats, psychological coercion, abuse of the legal process, deception, or other coercive means to compel someone to work." Most modern-day slavery occurs in labor-intensive, under-regulated industries, including agriculture and fishing, manufacturing and packaging, domestic work, and prostitution and sexual exploitation.

According to the International Labour Organization, as many as 24.9 million people around the world are in forced labor conditions, and one in every four victims are children, with women and girls being 99 percent of victims of sexual exploitation and 58 percent in other sectors. In addition to women and children, members of ethnic and religious minorities, refugees, and migrants are all at a greater risk of being forced into labor.

Though forced labor and slavery are associated with physical violence and intimidation, need and societal norms affect the rates of exploitation as well. And when unstable economies, lack of access to education, and poverty persist, opportunists strike.

The tendency is to also think that modern-day slavery only takes place in low- and middle-income countries (LMICs), but forced labor exists in higher-income countries as well, with cases of domestic servitude and commercial sexual exploitation being two of the most prevalent forms of forced labor in the United States and Europe. LGBTQ teens, runaways, and the homeless are also disproportionally targeted by traffickers.

Gender biases, low education levels, high rates of unemployment, and lax laws all make individuals and communities vulnerable to forced labor. But the engine that drives the illegal practice is consumption.

THE ECONOMIC IMPACT OF GLOBAL WARMING AND CLIMATE CHANGE

Scientists overwhelmingly believe that human activities have driven global warming, the long-term heating of Earth's climate system, and climate change, the long-term change in weather patterns. Historic flooding, melting polar ice caps, and forest fires are all real effects of the two phenomena. But there's an economic price to pay, too.

Since 1980, the United States alone has experienced more than 270 weather and climate disasters whose damages (according to the National Centers for Environmental Information) have exceeded $1 billion, with a total cost of $1.825 trillion. Rising temperatures could lead to declines in GDP and food supplies, even as prices rise and rural and urban labor markets see huge job losses.

Scientists believe that reducing the number of cars on the roads, improving infrastructure, and cutting down fewer trees can all contribute to reducing the effects of global warming and climate change.

The demand for fast fashion—cheap, trendy clothing—has manufactures looking for less expensive sources of labor. Cell phone batteries require cobalt mined by children in toxic environmental settings. And food items such as seafood and chocolate are also a part of the global production chain that results in the use of forced labor. The economic crime of forced labor not only has devastating effects on its victims and the communities from which they originate, but on the overall economy as well.

Private households that use forced labor are estimated to save approximately $8 billion annually by either underpaying taxes or not paying them at all. Construction, manufacturing, and mining activities earn an estimated $34 billion annually from forced labor. But by far, the highest profit from forced labor comes from sexual exploitation—a direct result of the demand and the price clients are willing to pay.

Activist Kevin Bales, who studies modern-day slavery, notes that when enslaved people are freed, the local economy improves because spending increases. In addition, he found that economies that used forced labor had major environmental issues. As globalization increases, the use of forced labor may continue, but addressing unemployment and poverty by increasing income and education around the world will help begin to address some of these issues.

– THE ECONOMIC IMPACT – OF SYSTEMATIC RACISM

Throughout history, systematic or structural racism has had a devastating effect on individuals and families. Chattel slavery and later Jim Crow laws ensured that Black people in America were concentrated in occupations that undervalued their labor. The abolition of slavery in 1863 did not automatically result in equal economic standing across races. Even the passage of the New Deal's Fair Labor Standards Act of 1938 (FLSA), which established the federal minimum wage and improved working conditions for white workers, largely excluded African Americans from receiving benefits because it exempted many domestic, agricultural, and service occupations. Even today, African American, Latino, and Asian people remain overrepresented in the lowest-paying domestic and service occupations.

Though redlining, the practice banks and the real estate industry used to outline neighborhoods where people of color lived, was banned in 1968, the practice still persists to some degree today, and has resulted in Black families and other people of color being unable to accrue wealth at the same rate as their white counterparts. The Federal Reserve reports that the net worth of the typical white family in the United States is ten times that of a Black family. Lower home values result in a lower tax base, which translates into fewer tax dollars for schools, teachers, and communities.

In his 1971 book *Economics of Discrimination*, Nobel laureate Gary Becker wrote that discrimination from a number of factors reduces the real income of both its target and the perpetrator. Harvard economists have found that it's much more difficult for Black children in low-income households in the United States to reach higher income brackets than for white children, and that environmental conditions such as racial bias is the reason why.

Racism doesn't only affect its direct victims; it affects the economy as a whole as well. In an August 2019 report, U.S.-based management consulting firm

McKinsey & Company wrote that the "persistent racial wealth gap in the United States is a burden on Black Americans as well as the overall economy." Today, almost 70 percent of middle-class Black children will fall out of the middle class as adults. This disparity will have an estimated cost of between $1 trillion and $1.5 trillion to the U.S. economy between 2019 and 2028. That's essentially costing $2,900 to $4,300 for every man, woman, and child in the United States. Without that wealth gap, GDP could be as much as 6 percent higher by 2028.

DR. PHYLLIS A. WALLACE (1921–1993)

Phyllis A. Wallace was born in Baltimore, Maryland, in 1921. She attended segregated schools growing up, and though she wanted to attend law school in Maryland, state law prohibited her from attending the all-white University of Maryland.

She would go on to attend New York University, where she received a BA in economics, and later attended Yale University, where she earned an MA and a PhD. She was the first woman to receive a doctorate of economics from Yale University.

Wallace later joined the National Bureau of Economic Research as an economist/statistician. She would later serve on the faculty of Atlanta University. In 1966, she began working for the Equal Employment Opportunity Commission, where she was the chief of technical studies from 1966 to 1969.

Wallace devoted much of her career to studying Black unemployment in the United States. In 1973, she helped with a precedent-setting legal decision against ATT, at the time the largest private employer in the United States. The lawsuit eventually resulted in a decision that ATT had discriminated against women and minority men. ATT agreed to pay millions in back wages.

Wallace is attributed with helping economists understand the role of Black women in the U.S. labor force.

CONCLUSION

Whether we consciously realize it or not, every day we interact with economic concepts, systems, and policies that influence every aspect of our daily lives. From the prices we pay for our groceries to drops in the interest rate that send us looking to refinance our mortgages, the impact of demand and supply, the factors of production, and monetary and fiscal policy on our lives can't be overlooked. Every decision we make as individuals, households, firms, and countries involves economic policies that have shaped our past and will mold our future. I hope *Everyday Economics Made Easy* has helped you gain a better understanding of what that future may hold.

— GLOSSARY —

Absolute Advantage: Occurs when an individual, firm, or country produces more output than another given the same amount of input.

Aggregate Demand: The total demand for goods and service at a specific price level and point in time in an economy.

Aggregate Supply: The total supply of goods and service at a given price level and point in time in an economy.

Antitrust Laws: Laws designed to limit monopolies in a market system.

Asset: An item of value from which its owner derives benefit.

Average Cost: The total cost of a company's outputs divided by the total number of units produced.

Bank: A financial institution where individuals and firms can invest or borrow money.

Behavioral Economics: A branch of economics that studies behavioral factors that affect decision making.

Bond: A loan that pays investors a fixed rate of return over a period of time.

Budget: An estimate of income and expenses over a period of time.

Budget Deficit: A budget deficit occurs when spending exceeds income.

Budget Surplus: A budget surplus occurs when income exceeds expenses.

Business Cycle: Fluctuations in economic growth over time.

Capital Good: Non-labor assets businesses use in the production process.

Capitalism: An economic system where private individuals and businesses, and not government, own capital goods.

Cartel: group of manufacturers who collude for the purpose of restricting competition and increasing prices.

Central Bank: A financial institution that controls a country's production and distribution of money.

Ceteris Paribus: A Latin phrase meaning "all other things being equal" used when explaining the laws of supply and demand to indicate that some components are being held constant.

Collateral: An asset pledged as security for a loan.

Commodities: The physical goods, such as gold, silver, and sugar, that are traded. May also mean any good produced for sale.

Communism: A political, social, and economic system characterized by the absence of social classes and public ownership of the factors of production.

Complementary Goods: Goods that are usually consumed together. Hot dogs and hot dog rolls and milk and cereal are examples.

Consumer Price Index (CPI): A measure of the average change in prices consumers pay over a time for a basket of consumer goods and services.

Consumer Theory: The study of how preferences and income affect consumer behavior.

Consumption: The household use of goods and services.

Cyclical Unemployment: A drop in employment caused by fluctuations in the economy.

Deflation: A decline in the prices for goods and services.

Demand Curve: The curve that illustrates the relationship between the price for a good and the quantity demanded of that good.

Demand Elasticity: The degree to which the quantity demanded changes when the price changes.

Demand Schedule: A table that illustrates the relationship between price and quantity demanded.

Diminishing Marginal Utility: The decrease in satisfaction a buyer receives from consuming an additional unit of a good or service.

Diminishing Returns: The decrease in incremental output of an item as a factor of its production increases incrementally.

Division of Labor: The division of the production process that enables people or groups to focus on specific tasks.

Economics: A social science that studies the allocation of scarce resources within a society.

Employment Rate: The ratio of the employed to the population of those of working age.

Entrepreneur: An individual who creates, organizes, and manages a business.

Entrepreneurship: One of the four factors of production that refers to the act of creating, organizing, and managing land, labor, and capital to create goods and services.

Excess Demand: A situation that occurs when buyers want more of a product at the current price than suppliers have available to sell.

Excess Supply: A situation that occurs when the quantity of goods supplied is greater than the quantity demanded at the current price.

Exchange Rate: The rate at which one country's currency is exchange for another.

Exports: Goods and services that are produced domestically and sold abroad.

Factors of Production: The inputs required to create a good or service. The four factors of production are land, labor, capital, and entrepreneurship.

Federal Funds Rate: The target interest rate set by the Federal Open Market Committee (FOMC).

Financial Market: A market where entities buy, sell, and trade assets.

Fiscal Policy: A government's tax and spending policy.

Fiscal Stimulus: Policy enacted by the government to address recession. Fiscal stimulus can include tax cuts or increased spending.

Full Employment: A level of employment when everyone willing and able to work is employed.

Globalization: The increasing integration and free flow of goods, investment, ideas, and labor across national boundaries.

Government Spending: The amount the government spends on goods and services.

Gross Domestic Product (GDP): A calculation of the value of all goods and services a country produces during a given period of time.

Hyperinflation: A rate of inflation that exceeds 50 percent per month.

Imports: Goods and services produced in one country and sold domestically.

Income: Money received by an individual or business.

Income Elasticity of Demand (YED): The positive correlation between income and the demand for normal goods.

Inflation: An economic state where prices are generally rising.

Inflation Rate: A measure of the change in the Consumer Price Index on a month-to-month and year-to-year basis.

Intellectual Property Rights: Legal rights granted to the creation of intellectual property. They include patents, copyrights, and trademarks.

Interest: The cost of borrowing money.

Interest Rate: The cost of borrowing money expressed as a percentage of the loan balance.

Invisible Hand: The unseen force in a society's market that pushes demand and supply toward equilibrium.

Laissez-faire: A French expression meaning "let it be." It is used to describe the belief that the government should not interfere with the economic function of a society.

Law of Demand: An economic principle that states that when all other things are equal, as a price of an item increases, consumers will demand less of that item.

Law of Supply: An economic principle that states that when all other things are equal, as a price of an item increases, the quantity supplied of that item will also increase.

Macroeconomics: The branch of economics that studies the activity of a society.

Marginal Cost: The additional cost incurred by producing one additional unit of a good or service.

Marginal Utility: The added satisfaction of happiness a buyer receives from consuming an additional unit of a good or service.

Market: A place where parties exchange things of value.

Market Economy: An economic system characterized by unrestricted competition among businesses.

Market Equilibrium: The point where the supply and demand curves cross, illustrating a balance where prices are stable.

Microeconomics: The field of economics that studies the way individuals, households, workers, and businesses make decisions and allocate scarce resources.

Monetary Policy: Policies implemented by the Central Bank to influence the amount of money and credit in the United States.

Monopolistic Competition: A form of imperfect competition where low barriers to entry result in many firms producing and offering similar products and services.

Monopoly: A form of imperfect competition where one company dominates the market.

National Debt: The amount of money the federal government owes its debtors.

Necessity Goods: Normal goods for which the elasticity of demand is between zero and one.

Nominal Interest Rate: The interest rate before inflation is taken into account.

Nominal Wage: The average hourly wage rate measured in dollars.

Nondurable Good: A good that is consumed immediately and only once and has a life span of less than three years. Food and clothing are nondurable goods.

Non-rival Good: A non-scarce good whose consumption does not reduce another's ability to consume.

Oligopoly: A market where a small number of firms dominate an industry.

Opportunity Cost: The forfeited potential gain from choosing one option over another.

Price Elasticity of Demand: The relationship between the quantity demanded of a product and a change in its price.

Price Elasticity of Demand = % Change in Quantity Demanded / % Change in Price

Price Fixing: When a firm in an oligopoly sets prices and others follow.

Production Possibilities Curve: A curve that shows the combinations of output that will occur when two goods are produced that use the same set of resources.

Property Rights: Laws that give entities exclusive, enforceable, and transferable ownership of resources.

Quantity Demanded: How much of a good consumers demand at a certain price point.

Rational Choice Theory: A theory that assumes that in situations of scarcity, individuals always choose the option that maximizes their well-being and satisfaction.

Real Interest Rate: The rate an entity receives adjusted for inflation.

Real Wage: Wages that have been adjusted for inflation. The nominal wage, adjusted to take into account the changes in prices between different time periods. It measures the amount of goods and services the worker can buy. See also: Nominal Wage.

Recession: When the country experiences two or more consecutive quarters of economic decline as measured by GDP and unemployment figures.

Scarcity: The gap between what we want to consume and what's available for consumption.

Stagflation: Five or more quarters of negative GDP growth.

Stock Exchange: A financial marketplace where stocks are offered for sale to the public.

Subprime Mortgage: Residential mortgages extended to high-risk or "subprime" customers with poor credit histories.

Supply Curve: Illustrates how the quantity of a good supplied will respond to various prices over time.

Supply Schedule: A table that shows the relationship between price and quantity supplied.

Tariff: A tax levied on imported goods.

Tax: Compulsory fees levied on corporations and individuals by a governing body.

Trade Deficit: A trade imbalance where a country's imports exceed its exports.

Trade Surplus: A trade imbalance where a country's exports exceed its imports.

Unemployment: A situation where someone who is willing and able to work is unable to find work.

Unemployment Rate: The level of unemployment in the labor force expressed as a percentage.

Utility: A measure economists use to measure happiness.

Veblen Goods: Goods or services that signify high social ranking and wealth.

— REFERENCES —

"30 Things You Didn't Know About Your Favorite Childhood Cereals." Cheapism, https://blog.cheapism.com/breakfast-cereal-facts.

Activities of U.S. Multinational Enterprises: 2016. U.S. Bureau of Economic Analysis (BEA), https://www.bea.gov/news/2018/activities-us-multinational-enterprises-2016.

Bureau, U.S. Census. "Income and Poverty in the United States: 2019." U.S. Census Bureau, https://www.census.gov/library/publications/2020/demo/p60-270.html.

Carmody, Michelle. "What Caused Hyperinflation in Venezuela: A Rare Blend of Public Ineptitude and Private Enterprise." The Conversation, http://theconversation.com/what-caused-hyperinflation-in-venezuela-a-rare-blend-of-public-ineptitude-and-private-enterprise-102483.

Desjardins, Jeff. "The World's 20 Most Profitable Companies." Visual Capitalist, October 21, 2019, https://www.visualcapitalist.com/the-worlds-20-most-profitable-companies.

"Economic Ideas of Kautilya (With Critical Estimate)." Economics Discussion, May 23, 2016, https://www.economicsdiscussion.net/articles/economic-ideas-of-kautilya-with-critical-estimate/21140.

"Economic Scarring: The Long-Term Impacts of the Recession." Economic Policy Institute, https://www.epi.org/publication/bp243.

Editors, History com. "The Roaring Twenties." HISTORY, https://www.history.com/topics/roaring-twenties/roaring-twenties-history.

Forced Labour, Modern Slavery and Human Trafficking, https://www.ilo.org/global/topics/forced-labour/lang--en/index.htm.

"Global Poverty: Facts, FAQs, and How to Help." World Vision, October 16, 2020, https://www.worldvision.org/sponsorship-news-stories/global-poverty-facts.

Glover, Julian, and Ken Miguel. "What Are Structural, Institutional and Systemic Racism?" ABC7 San Francisco, July 10, 2020, https://abc7news.com/6292530.

"History of Economic Thought." New World Encyclopedia, https://www.newworldencyclopedia.org/entry/History_of_economic_thought.

"Income Inequality." Inequality.Org, https://inequality.org/facts/income-inequality.

"Intellectual Property Enforcement." U.S. Department of State, https://www
.state.gov/intellectual-property-enforcement.

"Janet Yellen: Biography, the Fed, & Facts." *Encyclopedia Britannica*, https://www
.britannica.com/biography/Janet-Yellen.

"John Stuart Mill." Econlib, https://www.econlib.org/library/Enc/bios/Mill.html.

Koba, Mark. Consumer Price Index: CNBC Explains, August 4, 2011, https://www
.cnbc.com/id/43769766.

"Mises Library." Mises Institute, https://mises.org/library/it-all-began-usual-
greeks.

OPEC : Our Mission. https://www.opec.org/opec_web/en/about_us/23.htm.

"Overview." World Bank, https://www.worldbank.org/en/topic/poverty
/overview.

Poverty Facts. https://www.povertyusa.org/facts. Accessed July 22, 2021.

"Poverty Guidelines." ASPE, https://aspe.hhs.gov/topics/poverty-economic-
mobility/poverty-guidelines.

"Property Rights." Econlib, https://www.econlib.org/library/Enc/PropertyRights
.html.

Reuell, Peter, and Harvard Staff. "Harvard Study Shows Exactly How Poverty
Impacts Children's Success." *Harvard Gazette*, May 17, 2019, https://news
.harvard.edu/gazette/story/2019/05/harvard-study-shows-exactly-how-
poverty-impacts-childrens-success.

"Ruth Wakefield & the Chocolate-Chip Cookie." *New England Today*, December 8,
2014, https://newengland.com/yankee-magazine/living/trivia/close-ruth-
wakefield-chocolate-chip-cookie.

Shaftel, Holly. "Overview: Weather, Global Warming and Climate Change."
Climate Change: Vital Signs of the Planet, https://climate.nasa.gov/resources
/global-warming-vs-climate-change.

Smith, Adam B. U.S. Billion-Dollar Weather and Climate Disasters, 1980 - Present
(NCEI Accession 0209268). NOAA National Centers for Environmental
Information, 2020, doi:10.25921/STKW-7W73.

"The Economic Impacts of Counterfeiting and Piracy." ICC - International
Chamber of Commerce, https://iccwbo.org/publication/economic-impacts-
counterfeiting-piracy-report-prepared-bascap-inta.

"The Economics of Discrimination." Econlib, https://www.econlib.org/library
/Columns/y2010/Murphydiscrimination.html.

"The Poverty Rates for Every Group in the US: From Age and Sex to Citizenship Status." *USA Today*, https://www.usatoday.com/story/money/2019/11/06/united-states-poverty-rate-for-every-group/40546247.

Wages and the Fair Labor Standards Act. U.S. Department of Labor, https://www.dol.gov/agencies/whd/flsa.

"What Are the Sources of Revenue for the Federal Government?" Tax Policy Center, https://www.taxpolicycenter.org/briefing-book/what-are-sources-revenue-federal-government.

"What Is Modern Slavery?" U.S. Department of State, https://www.state.gov/what-is-modern-slavery/.

"Why Modern-Day Slavery Is a Drag on the Economy and Environment." KGOU, October 17, 2014, https://www.kgou.org/world/2014-10-17/why-modern-day-slavery-is-a-drag-on-the-economy-and-environment.

"Women's Economic Agenda: Creating an Economy That Works for Everyone." Economic Policy Institute, https://www.epi.org/womens agenda.

— ACKNOWLEDGMENTS —

Contrary to popular opinion, writing is not a solitary activity. Behind every draft and round of revisions is a team of friends, family, and editors who help to encourage, support, and shape a bundle of words into a book. Eternal thanks to my parents and sisters for their unending support. Thanks to friends and family who constantly cheerlead my writing. To John, Katie, and the team at Quarto, thanks for your wonderful guidance on this project. And finally, much gratitude to Christa, Yas, and the entire team of wonderful editors and writers at Tessera Editorial.

— ABOUT THE AUTHOR —

Grace Wynter is a writer and freelance editor. She holds a BBA in economics, an MBA in marketing from Georgia State University, and a certificate in editing from the University of Chicago. Grace is a regular contributor to Writer Unboxed—a Writer's Digest Best of the Best Websites for Writers—and her work has been featured on CNN.com and the *Huffington Post*. When she's not alternating between the Marvel and DC universes, she resides in Atlanta, Georgia.

B

basic principles
  cartels, 38
  factors of production, 31
  imperfect competition,
    35
  intellectual property
    rights, 30
  macroeconomics, 24,
    25, 26
  market structures, 34–40
  microeconomics, 24,
    25, 26
  monopolies, 36
  monopolistic
    competition, 37
  oligopolies, 37–38
  perfect competition, 35
  profit, 33–34
  property rights, 29–30
  rivalry, 28–29
  scarcity, 26, 27
biographies. See also
    history.
  Aquinas, Thomas, 67
  Friedman, Milton, 86
  Keynes, John Maynard,
    96
  Locke, John, 75
  Marx, Karl, 21
  Mill, John Stuart, 46
  Quesnay, François, 39
  Smith, Adam, 12
  Wallace, Phyllis A., 127
  Yellen, Janet, 101

C

consumer theory
  buying behavior, 70
  consumer price index
    (CPI), 88
  consumer price inflation,
    89
  definition of, 68
  extended decision-
    making, 70
  impulse buying, 70
  law of diminishing
    marginal utility,
    71–72
  limited decision-making,
    70
  marginal utility, 69
  middle-class growth, 73
  permanent income and,
    86
  poverty and, 73–75
  rational choice theory, 68
  Roaring Twenties, 84
  routine response, 70
  total utility, 69
  utility, 69, 71–72
  utils, 69, 71
  worldwide consumption
    expenditure, 68
costs
  average hourly
    compensation, 32
  consumer price index
    (CPI), 88
  cost-push inflation, 87
  economies of scale and,
    36
  globalization and, 17
  inflation and, 99
  labor, 31, 66, 120
  marginal cost, 43
  market economies, 20, 34
  neoclassical economics
    and, 14
  opportunity cost, 43, 46
  outsourcing and, 120
  price ceilings, 65
  price controls, 65
  price floors, 22, 65
  price theory, 86
  supply curve and, 62–63

D

demand
  anticipated price and, 50
  availability of substitute
    products and, 50
  complementary goods,
    49
  definition of, 48
  demand curve, 52, 54, 55
  demand schedule, 51, 54
  demand shifters, 49
  determinants of demand,
    49
  drivers of, 49–50
  elasticity of demand, 50,
    52, 54–55, 58
  equilibrium price, 63–65
  excess demand, 65
  income elasticity of
    demand (YED), 56
  inelastic demand, 55
  inferior goods, 56, 57
  law of demand, 51
  luxury goods, 56
  market equilibrium,
    63–65
  necessity goods, 56
  non-price factors, 55
  normal goods, 56
  personal preference and,
    49, 50
  price, 50
  price elasticity of
    demand, 51
  quantity demanded, 48
  recession and, 94
  status symbols, 57
  T&K Bakery example,
    51–52, 54, 55
  Veblen goods, 57
  wages and, 49, 56
depressions
  definition of, 95
  government response to,
    95–96, 102
  Great Depression, 14,
    95–96, 102, 114
  minimum wage and, 66
  recession and, 94, 95

E

economic policy. See also
    Federal Reserve
    System (FRS);
    government.
  contractionary fiscal
    policies, 102
  coupon payments, 103
  definition of, 97
  dual mandate, 97
  expansionary fiscal
    policies, 103
  federal funds rate, 99
  fiscal policy, 97, 102–104
  fixed-income securities,
    103
  monetary policy, 97, 99,
    100, 102
  stocks, 110–116
  Treasury bills, 103

Treasury bonds
(T-bonds), 103
Treasury notes, 103
economic systems
command economies,
18–20
market economies, 20–21
Marxian economics /
Marxism, 13, 21
mixed economies, 22
traditional economies, 18
employment. *See* labor.
everyday economics
demand, 50
diminishing marginal
utility, 69
expansionary monetary
policy, 100
inferior goods, 57
macroeconomics, 26
microeconomics, 26
perfect competition, 35
price leadership, 39
rivalry, 28
structural unemployment
and, 120
total utility, 69
utility, 69

F

factors of production
capital / capital goods,
31, 33
entrepreneurship, 33
labor, 31–32, 41
land / natural resources,
31
Federal Reserve System
(FRS). *See also*
economic policy;
government.
budget deficits and, 107
contractionary monetary
policy, 100, 102
depression and, 95
expansionary monetary
policy, 100

Federal Open Market
Committee
(FOMC), 98
Federal Reserve Banks,
98
Federal Reserve Board
(FRB), 98
function of, 97, 99
history of, 97
inflation target, 99
monetary policy, 97–99,
104

G

globalization
definition of, 16
examples of, 15
government response
to, 17
low- and middle-income
countries (LMICs),
16, 73, 124
middle-class growth
and, 73
government. *See also*
economic policy;
Federal Reserve
System (FRS).
Affordable Care Act
(ACA), 105, 106
antitrust laws, 38, 40
budget deficits, 102, 107
Bureau of Labor Statistics
(BLS), 32, 76, 87,
88, 117, 123
Children's Health
Insurance Program
(CHIP), 105, 106
communism, 13, 19, 20,
21
Coronavirus Aid, Relief,
and Economic
Security (CARES)
Act, 104
defense spending, 105,
106
depressions and, 95–96,
102
Fair Labor Standards Act
(FLSA), 66, 125

Federal Deposit
Insurance
Corporation (FDIC),
96
fiscal policies, 17, 25, 97,
102–104, 107, 123
globalization and, 16–17
Great Depression and,
95–96, 102
gross domestic product
(GDP) and, 76–78,
81, 83, 105–106
inflation and, 14, 77, 82,
87–89, 90, 95, 97,
99, 102, 103, 107
interest on debt, 107
Keynesian economics
and, 8, 14
laissez-faire economics,
10, 11, 21
libertarianism and, 11
market economies, 20
market equilibrium and,
65
Marxian economics and,
13
Medicaid, 105, 106
Medicare, 105, 106, 108
mercantilism and, 9
minimum wage, 22, 65,
66, 125
mixed economies, 21, 22
monetarism, 14, 86
money and, 86
North American Free
Trade Agreement
(NAFTA), 81
North Korea, 19, 20
poverty, 73–74, 107
price floors, 22, 65
recession and, 92
Securities and Exchange
Commission (SEC),
111
social safety net
programs, 107
Social Security, 105, 106,
107, 108
Soviet Union, 20
spending, 105–107

Supplemental Nutrition
  Assistance Program
  (SNAP), 74, 118
taxes, 108, 109
Troubled Asset Relief
  Program (TARP),
  94
US-Mexico-Canada
  Agreement
  (USMCA), 81
gross domestic product
  (GDP)
business cycle and, 82, 83
calculation of, 76–77
climate change and, 124
definition of, 76
depression and, 95
government and, 76–78,
  81, 83, 105–106
income inequality and,
  118, 127
investments, 78
monetarism and, 14
net exports, 78–79
North Korea, 19
outsourcing and, 81
personal consumption
  expenditures, 78
recession and, 91, 92
stagflation, 92
systemic racism and, 127
wages and, 77

H

history. *See also*
  biographies.
ancient Egypt, 8
classical liberalism, 11
consumption function
  theory, 14
early economic thought
  (750–275 BCE),
  8–9
Great Depression, 14, 95,
  102, 114
Keynesian economics,
  13–14
"invisible hand," 12
laissez-faire economics,
  10, 11
libertarianism, 11

mainstream economics,
  16
Marxian economics /
  Marxism, 13, 21
mercantilism, 9
Middle Ages, 9
monetarism, 14
neoclassical economics,
  14
New World, 16
physiocracy, 10–11
Silk Road, 16
stock exchanges, 110
usury, 9
utilitarianism, 13

I

income. *See* wages.
inflation
  consumer price index
    (CPI), 88
  consumer price inflation,
    89
  cost-push inflation, 87
  definition of, 87
  demand-pull inflation,
    87
  government and, 14, 77,
    82, 87–89, 90, 95,
    97, 99, 102, 103, 107
  hyperinflation, 89, 90
  individual effect of, 89
  measuring, 87–89
  nominal income, 89
  real income, 89

L

labor. *See also* wages.
  as factor of production, 31
  costs of, 31, 66, 120
  Fair Labor Standards Act
    (FLSA), 66
  recession and, 94
  Roaring Twenties, 84
  T&K Bakery example, 119
  unemployment, 117,
    119–121

M

macroeconomics
  bear market, 83
  boom and bust cycle, 82
  bull market, 82
  business cycle, 82
  contraction phase, 83
  deflation, 90
  depression, 95–96
  economic development,
    80
  expansion phase, 82
  gross domestic product
    (GDP), 76–79, 83
  international trade, 79
  peak, 82
  recession, 91–95
  trade cycle, 82
  trade deficits, 80
  trade surpluses, 79
  trough phase, 83
  unemployment and, 117
market structure
  cartels, 38
  definition of, 34
  economies of scale, 36
  imperfect competition,
    36
  monopoly, 36
  oligopolies, 37–40
  perfect competition, 35
  price fixing, 38
  price leadership, 38, 39
microeconomics. *See*
    consumer theory;
    demand; supply.
money. *See also* wages
  categorization, 85
  definition of, 85
  government and, 86
  M1 category, 85
  M2 category, 85
  monetary base, 85
  money supply, 85
  price / value relationship,
    86

P

production possibilities
    curve (PPC)
  definition of, 41
  diminishing returns, 43

marginal cost, 43
opportunity cost, 43, 46
production possibilities
table, 42–43
T&K Bakery example,
41–45

R

recession
COVID-19 and, 91, 92, 121
definition of, 91
demand and, 94
expansionary policies,
103
government and, 92, 103
Great Recession, 92,
93–94, 100
labor and, 94
scarring, 95
signs of, 94
societal impact of, 94–95
subprime mortgage
crisis, 92, 93–94
timeline, 92

S

salaries. See wages.
societal impact
climate change, 124
cyclical unemployment,
119
ethnic diversity, 123
frictional unemployment,
119
gender pay gap, 122–123
generosity, 126
income inequality, 118
natural unemployment,
120
outsourcing, 120
poverty, 73–75
recession, 94–95
slavery (forced labor),
123–125
structural
unemployment, 119
systemic racism, 125–127
unemployment, 117,
119–121
women in, 122–123, 123
stocks
bear market, 83, 115

Black Monday, 114
Black Tuesday, 114
bull market, 82, 115
common stock, 110
corrections, 115
definition of, 110
dividends, 110
Dow Jones Industrial
Average (Dow), 114
economy compared to,
113
equity financing, 111
exchanges, 110, 111, 115,
116
gross domestic product
(GDP) and, 78
initial public offerings
(IPOs), 111, 112
investment bankers, 111
as liquid assets, 113
market indexes, 114–115
National Association
of Securities
Dealers Automated
Quotations
(NASDAQ)
exchange, 115
New York Stock Exchange
(NYSE), 110, 115
ownership of, 113–114
performance factors, 113
portfolio managers, 111
preferred stock, 110
quotes, 116
Roaring Twenties, 84
Securities and Exchange
Commission (SEC)
and, 111
S&P 500, 115
stockbrokers, 111
stock market, 111, 113, 115
supply and demand, 115
unemployment and, 121
supply
equilibrium price, 63–65
excess supply, 65
law of supply, 59
market equilibrium,
63–65
non-price factors, 62–63
price ceilings, 65
price controls, 65
price floors, 65

production costs and,
62–63
Simon Sews example,
59–61, 62–63,
63–64
supply curve, 60–61, 62
supply schedule, 59

T

trade
deficits, 80
exports, 9, 77, 78–80,
81, 90
imports, 77, 78, 79–80,
81, 90
international trade, 79
North American Free
Trade Agreement
(NAFTA), 81
surpluses, 79
trade cycle, 82
US-Mexico-Canada
Agreement
(USMCA), 81

W

wages. See also labor;
money.
401k plans, 108
as driver of demand, 49
average compensation
costs, 32
demand and, 49, 56
expansion and, 82
gross domestic product
(GDP) and, 77
income elasticity of
demand (YED), 56
income inequality, 118,
127
interest rates and, 99
minimum wage, 22, 65,
66, 125
nominal income, 89
outsourcing and, 81
permanent income, 86
poverty, 73–75
real income, 89
recession scarring and,
95
systemic racism and, 127
taxes, 108